# RISE
### AND
# SHINE

# RISE
# AND
# SHINE

An Astrological Guide
to How You Show Up
in the World

## CHRISTOPHER
## RENSTROM

a TarcherPerigee book

**tarcher**perigee
an imprint of Penguin Random House LLC
penguinrandomhouse.com

Most TarcherPerigee books are available at special quantity discounts for bulk
purchase for sales promotions, premiums, fund-raising, and educational needs.
Special books or book excerpts also can be created to fit specific needs.
For details, write: SpecialMarkets@penguinrandomhouse.com.

Library of Congress Cataloging-in-Publication Data

Names: Renstrom, Christopher, author.
Title: Rise and shine: an astrological guide to how you
show up in the world / Christopher Renstrom.
Description: [New York, New York]: TarcherPerigee, an imprint of
Penguin Random House LLC, [2022] | "A TarcherPerigee book."
Identifiers: LCCN 2022017483 (print) | LCCN 2022017484 (ebook) |
ISBN 9780525541103 (trade paperback) | ISBN 9780525541110 (epub)
Subjects: LCSH: Ascendant (Astrology) | Interpersonal relations—Miscellanea.
Classification: LCC BF1717.R36 2022 (print) | LCC BF1717 (ebook) |
DDC 133.5—dc23/eng/20220716
LC record available at https://lccn.loc.gov/2022017483
LC ebook record available at https://lccn.loc.gov/2022017484

Printed in the United States of America
1st Printing

Book design by Laura K. Corless

To Michael Lutin—my role model, mentor, and friend

# CONTENTS

## PART 1

# First Impressions: Your Rising Sign

The Rising Sign is one of the most important features of your astrological chart. It ranks right up there with the Sun and the Moon. But unlike the Sun and the Moon, the Rising Sign is not a planet. It's a demarcation line. It marks the fixed point on the eastern horizon where night becomes day so that whatever zodiac sign was "rising" there at the time of your birth becomes your Rising Sign.

Your Sun Sign describes who you are. It's everything that you know about yourself to be true. Some of these characteristics you're proud of. And others? Maybe not so much. Nevertheless they're the personality traits that you identify with the most.

Your Moon Sign describes your emotional life. It's how you *really* feel about things deep down inside. The planet of habits, memories, and dreams, the Moon remembers you even when you've forgotten yourself. The Moon is also where you turn to when you feel unsafe.

Your Rising Sign is the face of your astrological chart. It's not a mask, a

**Your Rising Sign is the face of your astrological chart.** persona, or a role that you play. It's your face—and it's every bit as spontaneous, expressive, and reactive as your physical face is.

Think about your face for a moment. Your face makes you recognizable as you. No two faces are exactly alike—even with identical twins. Each person's face is so individual and distinct that facial recognition is now the standard for unlocking your smartphone and authenticating payments. But who sees your face more during the course of a day—you or other people? It's other people. Now that might be hard to believe in an era of selfies and Zoom calls, but it's still other people who meet your gaze, sheepishly avoid eye contact, or don't even look up as you walk past because they don't know you from Adam. Like your face, your Rising Sign is continually registering the faces of others and responds accordingly. It decides what to reveal and what to conceal, independently of the rest of your horoscope.

We all have a pretty good idea of what our face looks like and what we hope to convey by it, but it's others' reactions to our expressions that influence our interactions. How many times has your thoughtful frown been misinterpreted as sullen and off-putting or your smile regarded as inviting when you're actually just being polite? Your Rising Sign is on show for everyone to see and it knows it. It's the first glimpse others get of you, and that includes your voice and demeanor. Everyone wants to make a good impression but oftentimes we can be in the dark about the signals we send or the vibes we put across. All of this is bound up in the zodiac sign people meet first, and not the one you truly are.

# ASTROLOGY IS A CALENDAR

There are two ways of telling time—a calendar and a clock. The calendar tells you what day it is while the clock tells you the hour, and that's precisely what the Sun Sign and the Rising Sign do. The Sun Sign will always tell you the time of year that someone was born while the Rising Sign will tell you the time of day. Here's how it works.

In Astrology we work with a 360-degree circle that is divided into twelve signs just like our calendar is divided into twelve months. This circle is called a horoscope.

The Earth orbits the Sun in a counterclockwise direction. The Earth's orbit around the Sun gives us the seasons. Now in Astrology, everything is seen from the Earth's point of view so it's not the Earth that orbits the Sun, but rather the Sun that orbits *us*. As the Sun moves through the signs in a year—the Sun is in Aries in April, Taurus in May, Gemini in June, and so on—you will see it move in the direction mapped out on the figure below. The Sun in a zodiac sign will always tell you what time of year it is.

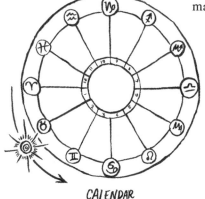

CALENDAR

The Earth orbits the Sun in a counterclockwise direction so the order of the signs is counterclockwise.

3

# ASTROLOGY IS ALSO A CLOCK

As the Earth orbits the Sun, it also rotates on its axis. The Earth's rotation on its axis gives us day and night. The side that faces the Sun is day, and the side that faces away is night. The Earth rotates on its axis in the same counterclockwise direction, from west to east, yet the Earth's rotation is also what creates the illusion of the Sun moving in a *clockwise* direction. This is why the Sun rises in the morning on the left, moves across the sky, and then sets on the right at night. Remember that everything in Astrology is seen from the Earth's point of view and that's how the Sun looks to us in the sky during the day.

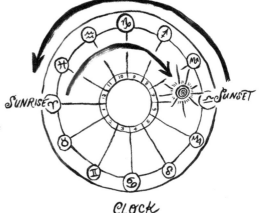

The Earth rotates on its axis from west to east, creating the illusion of the Sun moving clockwise.

Let's say that you were born on March 23. An Astrologer would immediately know that you are an Aries because the Sun is in the astrological sign of Aries from March 20 to April 18. But let's say that you were born at seven thirty in the morning. Then the Astrologer would hazard a guess that you're probably an Aries Rising because you were born around Sunrise. That would make you an Aries/Aries Rising because the Sun in Aries is rising over the horizon line on the left. Anyone born at Sunrise has their own zodiac sign rising.

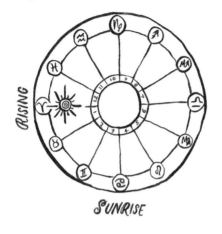

If you're an Aries born at dawn, then you are an Aries/Aries Rising.

SUNRISE

Now let's say that your birthday is March 23, but you were born at noon. You're still an Aries because it's still the same day, but the time has changed. You now are a Cancer Rising because Cancer was the zodiac sign that was rising over the horizon when you were born.

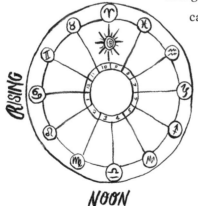

If you're an Aries born at noon, then you are an Aries/Cancer Rising.

NOON

What if you're an Aries born around Sunset? Then you are an Aries with Libra Rising. This can be a challenging placement because the Sun is as far away as it can be from the Ascendant. People are more likely to register you as a Libra because that's the sign they "see" first.

If you're an Aries born at Sunset, then you are an Aries/Libra Rising.

SUNSET

And if you're an Aries born around midnight? Then you are an Aries with Capricorn Rising. As you can see, the wheel has turned full circle so that with the dawn of a new day Aries will once again be rising over the horizon along with the Sun.

If you are an Aries born at midnight, then you are an Aries/Capricorn Rising.

Midnight

# FINDING YOUR RISING SIGN

The simplest way to find your Rising Sign is to input your birthday and time into an Astrology website or app. To deepen your understanding of how it works, here's a brief explanation. There are twenty-four hours in a day and twelve signs in the zodiac. Remember how the year is divided into twelve months, with each month corresponding to a zodiac sign? Well, each sign gets two hours of the day allotted to it because 2 x 12 = 24. Think of the signs as affixed to a wheel that is slowly turning. This wheel mimics the rotation of the Earth so that for two hours every day each sign will rise over the horizon before it's replaced by the following sign in zodiacal order. If you were born between six and eight in the morning, then you were born when your Sun Sign was rising. If you were born between eight and ten in the morning, then you were born when the zodiac sign that *follows* your Sun Sign was rising. Between ten and noon and it's the sign that's two signs after your Sun Sign that's rising, and so on.

As you can imagine, birth times have their pluses and minuses. Being born at Sunrise makes you up close and personal but doesn't really lend itself to seeing yourself objectively, whereas being born at Sunset might make you so removed that others often feel like you're never around or just don't care. The Sun high in the chart is aspirational but can also create a disconnect between how people see you and who you want to be, while the Sun at the bottom of the chart is so rooted in place that people assume you will always be there for them, which is why they stopped asking you how you're doing a long time ago.

Ideally your Rising Sign helps to accomplish the things you want in life, but in some cases your Rising Sign may work against you—especially if it isn't connected to your Sun Sign by element, mode, or Ruling Planet. This is why some people say that they identify more with their Rising Sign than they do with their Sun Sign. In that scenario, there just isn't a strong tie between them—and since the Rising Sign is always on show for the world to see, then it's the Rising Sign (also known as the Ascendant) that gets all the recognition.

In the end, your Rising Sign describes the way people see you. It's your presence, body language, quirks, and demeanor all wrapped up into one. The more you understand your Rising Sign, the more you'll recognize the relationship between it and your Sun Sign. This gives you a more complete picture of how you come across in daily life as well as an indispensable tool for figuring out why people sometimes take things the wrong way. Understanding your Rising Sign allows you to own and direct the first impression you make on others so that the impression serves rather than defines you.

In the sections that follow, we'll look at the twelve Rising Signs of the zodiac—what each of these astrological faces looks like, how they shape and relate to each Sun Sign, and how they interact with other Rising Signs as we all move through the world. This isn't a book about passing judgment on ourselves or others—it's a guide to understanding and decoding the Rising Sign in your chart as well as the ones around you. It's only through insight and reflection that we can truly understand ourselves and our relationships with others.

## PART 2

# Your Unique Personality: Sun Sign/Rising Sun Combinations

## ARIES RISING

You need to be first. That's why you arrive early for appointments, answer before anyone else, and step forward when others hem and haw. You have to be out in front. Driven by an overriding sense of urgency, you won't put off for tomorrow what can be done in the next twenty minutes. You're direct, decisive, and get visibly impatient when kept waiting. You don't like following and if you find yourself standing behind someone in line who isn't moving as quickly as you think they should be, then you will push them to hurry things along.

People know to get out of your way. It's like pulling over to the side of the road to let an ambulance pass. You come on that strong. When you're an

**You came into the world with a mission.**

Aries Rising you feel like everything you do is crucial. It's why you won't think twice about telling a loved one to stop what they're doing and come help you out. Your thinking is: It won't take very long, what you're doing is much more important, and they can always pick up where they left off later. Aries Rising isn't exactly known for respecting others' priorities.

It hurts when people say you always have to win. It implies you're a sore loser—or worse, that you should throw the game just to let somebody else win for a change. First of all, you're an honest competitor. You don't believe in going easy on anyone. That would be cheating. Second, you don't do anything half-assed. You always give it your best shot. Aries is ruled by Mars, the gladiator planet, so you're only as good as your last thumbs-up. You attack everything you do as if your life depended on it.

Navigating gender roles is something you have to do constantly because Mars is still seen as the he-man planet. If you're a guy you're expected to "man up" when things get tough, and if you're a woman you're told to dial it back so that you don't come across as angry and off-putting. Luckily, upsetting people's expectations isn't too much of a problem for you, but it still smarts.

Aries Rising means you came into the world with a mission. You may not have the clearest idea of what it is, but you know that time's running out and lives are at stake. Maybe you're here to fight the good fight, advocate for those who have been beaten down, or do the one thing that nobody thought could be done. Whatever it is, you need to commit to it in full because anything less just won't cut it.

# ARIES SUN/ARIES RISING

Things matter when you're an Aries/Aries Rising. It's why you act on impulse and speak up when it would be wiser not to. You can't abide holding back or playing it safe. You were built to champion and defy. Quick to butt heads with bullies, haters, and shamers, you're an enemy of anyone who tries to make somebody else feel bad about who they are. You don't think twice about getting up in people's faces.

You know that you're rough around the edges. A work in progress, you're constantly struggling to get to that place in life where you can finally say you made it. Unfortunately, you can't escape this feeling that you may never get there. It sounds self-defeatist, but it's not. It's just that when you're convinced that you can do better there's no such thing as being the best. How can there be when you're always pushing limits, taking risks, and raising the bar?

It's easy to get a rise out of you. Your face turns red. And even if your skin complexion can hide the color, you still can't escape that telltale burning sensation. Your anger, embarrassment, or sexual excitement is on show for everyone to see. Now this could lead you to collect your things and make a hasty exit, but you know that if you did that then you would only have to face these people later, which is why you choose to wear your emotions proudly, like a scarlet letter. A moment's humiliation often turns into a triumph when you're an Aries/Aries Rising because you won't back down. You should never feel ashamed about showing that you care—especially when you can't help it.

People expect you to be a hero. They want you to save the day, fight the fights they don't want to fight, or fall on your sword if need be. Don't be a dupe. It's hard to resist the distress call when everything feels so heated and in the moment, but when you see that you're the one taking the hits for people sipping cocktails and cheering you on from a safe distance, then you'll realize the wisdom of letting them fight their own battles. And that's the moment when you turn the tables on those who were using you to their own ends.

# TAURUS SUN/ARIES RISING

You were born under the sign of the bull, Astrology's most territorial sign. You may not charge at people when they wander into your field, but you will tell them to keep away from your stuff or to stop asking if they can have a bite of what you're eating. You are hyper-protective when it comes to your things. You will even follow a best friend around your bedroom just to make sure that she doesn't go anywhere she's not supposed to. You're acutely aware of what's permissible and what's off-limits. And it's because you patrol your borders so vigilantly that people naturally turn to you to safeguard their interests. They can sleep at night knowing that you are on the job.

Rules get enforced, rents collected, and affairs managed uniformly when a Taurus Sun with Aries Rising is put in charge. There's a military efficiency to everything you do. You aren't afraid to have those uncomfortable conversations and your matter-of-fact approach turns issues into non-issues fast. You move so briskly and assertively that even recalcitrant types are reluctant to lock horns with you. This isn't the typical way that

Taurus Suns express themselves. They're usually more laid back and easy-going; however, it's the Aries Rising that makes you unrelenting.

But backing people into a corner is never a good idea. At some point they're bound to come out fighting. And the funny thing is this surprises you every time. It hurts your feelings. That's why it's important to introduce some give-and-take. Whether it's paying back a loan or meeting a deadline, you need to work with them and not against them. You aren't indulging bad habits by exploring alternatives or layaway plans. You're creating the means to an end that both sides will be happy with. Introducing some of that relaxed Taurus demeanor into your Aries Rising exchanges goes a long way.

Taurus is a Venus-ruled sign, which means that you're a sucker for a pretty face. It's sweet to see you get all gaga over someone but make sure that you know everything you need to know beforehand. Taurus Suns with Aries Rising can be remarkably naïve and focused on battling the dragon when they should be more wary of the damsel (or dude) in distress.

# GEMINI SUN/ARIES RISING

It's impossible to sit still. You have a million things going on at once. Not only does your mind move faster than most—always racing ahead, interrupting itself, switching topics and then doubling back again—but you have your fingers in so many pies that it's hard to remember which ones were yours in the first place. You're always becoming best friends with someone you just met, breaking up with somebody else you barely got to know, and picking fights with people who are on your side. You spar and feud like a boxing kangaroo. You can come across as manic, but those who know better understand that this is your way of enlivening things. You bore easily, so acting up can't be helped. Besides, your rib-poking, chain-yanking, and leg-pulling is all in fun.

Unfortunately, others don't always see it this way—especially authority figures who are often the butt of your jokes. You may succeed at getting them to laugh along with everyone else in the moment, but there's something about your Aries Rising that leaves them feeling burned, like there's a part of you that really enjoys besting them and taking them down a peg or two. For all of your Gemini tomfoolery, there's still a Mars-ruled Rising Sign that's playing for keeps. And the people who have been on the wrong side of this remember it. Resentment can build over time, which is why you want to check in to make sure that you haven't gone too far.

Gemini/Aries Risings make terrific buyers, sellers, and wheeler-dealers. You're results driven and excel in fast-changing, high-pressure environments. Geminis are already quick thinking because your Ruling Planet is Mercury, but that Aries Rising works like an accelerant. You can size up situations with the speed of a game-show contestant in the lightning round. You're the one who "kills it."

But living life on fast-forward means you naturally want to skip ahead. This can lead you to misjudge situations—or worse: never give them a chance to develop. You will never slow down but you can add a little more curiosity to your life by switching from exclamation points to question marks. Learn to let things unfold on their own and you may discover that people—and life—can surprise you.

# CANCER SUN/ARIES RISING

People think you're a lot tougher than you are. You have a brusque manner, a fuggedaboutit attitude, and will automatically shrug off any remark that's meant to irritate, provoke, or challenge. Your response to people looking for trouble is to ask: "Now why would you want to go and do something like that?" You have a natural talent for defusing situations. Your ability to combine sympathy with humor gets people to recognize a harebrained scheme for what it is—and you do this without ever making them feel foolish about it. A person of few words, others see you as strong and confident with nothing to prove. It's the perfect camouflage for someone born under the super sensitive sign of Cancer. Instead of your emotions being worn on your sleeve for everyone to see, you keep them tucked inside a drawer deep inside where you know that they're safe and secure.

You were born with conflicting impulses. The Aries Rising wants to stand up and fight while the Cancer Sun will go out of its way to avoid a confrontation. And in your case, the Cancer Sun often prevails because your Sun Sign is who you truly are. It takes a supreme act of self-control to not return fire, which is why you will withdraw when things get heated. People often misinterpret this as you beating a retreat, but you need some time away to compose yourself. Anger isn't something you can just let outside like a dog at night that has to do its business. You need to work through the hurt and the pain privately so that when you reemerge you'll be able to talk about things sensibly and constructively.

People see you as someone who can make a difference. It's why they come to you with all their hopeless plights. You may wonder where they got the idea that you even care, but it shows on your horoscopic face. And this is where the Rising Sign exerts its own special pull—even though it goes against your Sun Sign's instinct for self-preservation. An Aries Rising will always come through—no matter how many times you demur, beg off, or drag your feet. You have a hero's demeanor—and even reluctant heroes show up in the end.

# LEO SUN/ARIES RISING

You always get what you want. And it doesn't matter if you're rejected right away or the hiring agency says you're unqualified—you won't give up. You will focus your energies, improve your performance, and redouble your efforts until you succeed. Your passion and unabashed sincerity win over closed hearts so that even impossible-to-please types will make an exception and give you a chance. You have this ability to make people feel like choosing you is the best decision they could ever make.

You never disappoint. Your Aries Rising delivers on every promise and your Leo Sun won't make a promise it can't keep. But just because you don't disappoint doesn't mean you're immune to heartbreaks and setbacks. There have been a lot of letdowns. So many that it's hard to keep count. And you may be partially to blame. You've always had romantic notions, inflated expectations, and a naïve belief that if you can rise to the occasion then others will surely do the same, yet despite your efforts to see the best in people, your life is full of misplaced affections, jealous superiors, and lesser lights working to bring you down.

When you're a Leo/Aries Rising, no one can ever be as good as you. You're one of a kind. And this is fine when you're the athlete breaking records or the performer filling stadiums because it's all on you, but if you're a coach, director, or dance mom then it's up to someone else to deliver— and that's where things can get dicey. You're not always convinced that those you champion have what it takes. You will push them to push themselves, drive them to all their practices, and get them in to see the people who can really advance their careers, but there's a part of you that wonders if they really want it. Do they have the confidence? The pizzazz? Are they hungry enough?

And this is where you could benefit from some self-reflection. No one's ever going to do things the way you do them. That belongs to you, which means that what they do—along with all their good and bad choices— belongs to them. Support their spirit, guide their talent, safeguard their individuality, and you will give them the greatest gift of all: success in their own right.

# VIRGO SUN/ARIES RISING

The disappointment shows on your face. Whether it's a pained expression or an exasperated sigh, you can't hide your feelings of frustration when things don't turn out as expected. It's why nobody wants to partner with you in charades. You get so irritated when they fail to grasp the ingenious way that you are spelling out "Supercalifragilisticexpialidocious" that the entire room can sense the bitterness in your pantomime. And that's the difficulty with being a Virgo Sun with Aries Rising—you are forever surrounded by people who don't take things as seriously as you do and are ready to give up right when the going gets tough.

But just because you don't play well with others doesn't stop them from seeking your help. Everyone knows that you're the go-to person when it comes to solving an impossible problem or completing a demanding assignment. Not only are you proficient, but you make it all look easy. You'd be intimidating if it weren't for your love of teaching. At work, you will go to great lengths to show an associate or a team member how to do what you do. You live for that "aha" moment when the lightbulb goes off and puzzled frowns give way to an excited clarity. Training people to think for themselves turns them into peers, not dependents, and even prepares them to become creative collaborators one day.

Virgo/Aries Risings are famously single. And this isn't because you haven't found the right someone. What it stems from is your insistent self-sufficiency. Now, you'll say it's because nobody can do things as well as you can, but what's really going on is a refusal to rely on anyone but yourself. You don't want to be let down, which makes sense; however, being let down is how people grow close. How can you forgive if you're always in the right? Be understanding if you've got all the answers, or supportive if you don't know what it's like to stumble? Seeing others' faults and foibles shouldn't result in a rapid-fire checking off of boxes in the minus column; it should get you to open up and talk about your own. Come clean about who you are underneath that tightly wound exterior and you'll be able to breathe again. That's what true intimacy is all about.

# LIBRA SUN/ARIES RISING

People think you're from Mars, but you're really from Venus, which explains why they're always surprised to discover how nice you are once they get to know you. And truth to tell, you're surprised too because you never thought of yourself any other way. You're a Libra. You're fair-minded, even-tempered, and you get along with everybody, so why do people have such a hard time believing that?

When you're born at Sunset, like you were, then the Rising Sign becomes the only face that people see because the Sun's light is fading as it sinks below the horizon. It's as far away from the Ascendant as it can possibly be, which means that the *real* you just doesn't register at first.

What people see is someone who's direct, clear, and clipped. Famous for maintaining your cool under pressure, you're often called upon to take care of troubled situations. You're the one who restores order, explains the necessity of an unpopular rule, or escorts the freshly fired employee to the door. You're always polite and professional, unmoved and undeterred. Now you may see yourself as the opposite—a bundle of nerves who frets over every decision and is always on the verge of buckling—but nobody else sees that. Your Aries Rising won't let them. And this is what Rising Signs do—they cover for you in those moments when you are not being your best self.

Now when you were younger you probably had a wild side and butted heads with those in positions of authority on a regular basis, but over time you would have learned that getting angry harms you more than others. It's why you sought a healthy outlet for your aggression—in sports or the arts perhaps—and mastered the power of words, turning blind rage into poised debate. Libra is a civilizing sign and it prides itself on refinement. You're still easily roused—your Ascendant is ruled by Mars after all—but you keep it in check.

When you're a Libra Sun with Aries Rising, love and passion sometimes get the better of you. Rescuing one amour from a loveless union is romantic, but do it more than twice and it starts to look bad. You don't want to get a reputation for being a homewrecker.

# SCORPIO SUN/ARIES RISING

You're like the outlaw in a Hollywood Western who strides through the swinging doors unannounced. Suddenly the bustling saloon grows quiet as everyone watches you walk up to the bar. Nervously the bartender pours you a drink and whispers under his breath, "We don't want no trouble." You might permit a smile to slide across your lips as you take a long hard swallow. You intend to mind your own business and your back to the rest of the room broadcasts that it would be a good idea for others to mind their own business as well.

You're not unfriendly, but you're in no hurry to put people at ease either. When you're a Scorpio/Aries Rising you carry a pretty big chip on your shoulder. This stems from your childhood when you were made to feel unwelcome, laughed at, or found wanting. Scraped knees and bruised egos are all a part of life, but you never got over them. You were deeply hurt and have been pissed off about it since. Mars, named after the Roman god of war, rules both Scorpio and Aries so you're comfortable with anger. You like the way it makes you feel—bigger than your fears, tougher than your competition, an indomitable force in business.

A Scorpio Sun with Aries Rising is hot. You can't help it. It's why everyone wants to sleep with you, but you also need to be responsible. Passion plays fast and loose with your emotions and it's easy for sex to become revenge driven. Not in a physically abusive way, but in a "I'll show them" way. You may target people you think look down their noses at you so you can break their hearts before they break yours. This can become a vicious cycle with you caught in the loop if you're not careful.

Try softening your approach. It's not up to other people to break down your walls because you're like an impenetrable fortress. You'll exhaust them long before they exhaust you, which is why you have to do the brave thing and show some tenderness. This goes against everything in the Mars rule book, but there it is. It's ironic for someone who's been deeply hurt that it's up to you to show that you mean no harm in order to get along.

# SAGITTARIUS SUN/ARIES RISING

No one's going to tell you what you can and cannot do. You're your own person and you come and go as you please. Freedom means everything to you. That's why you're quick to assert yourself, won't think twice about thumbing your nose at authority, and are hell-bent on pushing limits. A larger-than-life personality who walks in without knocking, you have no problem taking the status quo by the collar and giving it a healthy shake.

People see you as a force to be reckoned with. Your Aries Rising makes you appear unstoppable and domineering. Luckily your Sagittarius Sun offsets that Mars-fueled combativeness. Sagittarius is a Jupiter-ruled sign, which means you're good-humored, benevolent, and generous in spirit. And since Mars was the foot solider to Jupiter, king of the gods in Roman mythology, it's your Sagittarius Sun that knows when to tell your Aries Rising to stand down. If years of heated responses and retaliatory attacks have taught you anything, it's that flying off the handle costs and oftentimes costs big.

Growing older and wiser is built into your Sun Sign/Rising Sign combination, as is your pioneering spirit and trailblazing fearlessness. You will always be out in front of the pack. And this is a good thing because you need lots of open space to roam when you're a Sagittarius/Aries Rising. You're drawn to the backwoods, deserts, and any other place that bears more than a passing resemblance to uncharted territory. However, being a trailblazer doesn't necessarily make you a leader. You enjoy being the first to do something nobody's ever tried before, but once it becomes standard fare you quickly lose interest. Now this could inspire you to become even more innovative, or you may simply choose to move on. You're not keen on seeing what was once wild and untamed devolve into something suburban and mundane.

You shy away from anything that hints at confinement, like a traditional relationship or corporate job. Startups, freelance gigs, and pop-up shops are where you prosper because you can make your own hours and create your own lifestyle. Few Sun Sign/Rising Sign combinations are as aspirational as yours. You may not have the clearest idea of what you're looking for in life, but you will always defend your right to go find it.

# CAPRICORN SUN/ARIES RISING

You always come out on top. It's incredible considering how the first part of your life was spent at the bottom of the barrel looking up. Early circumstances were challenging and prospects so limited that people who knew you then have a hard time reconciling you with who you are now, but the simple truth is you've always known that the only place to go is up. You also understand that any accomplishment is meaningless unless you earn it on your own.

When you're a Capricorn Sun with Aries Rising, everything has to be done the hard way. You have an uncanny ability to choose the toughest course, the longest struggle, and the steepest climb. Moreover, you will refuse any help. And it doesn't matter if a friend of a friend can open doors or trained experts can show you a more effective means, you are mulishly compelled to do things on your own from start to finish. It's how you discover and then familiarize yourself with the raw materials that will ultimately shape your success; a success that will work for you and *only* you. You are truly self-made.

Conflict with authority is built into your Sun Sign/Rising Sign combination. You're either struggling to impress someone who refuses to be impressed or you feel guilty about surpassing someone who means the world to you. Both impulses are tied to your father and could prove disastrous if left unsupervised. The first leads to setting the bar too high, resulting in burnout and resentment, while the second leads to setting the bar too low thereby limiting the scope of what you can achieve. The important thing for any Capricorn Sun/Aries Rising to learn is to be your own dad, to give yourself the approval, the recognition, and the tough-love talk when you need it. That goes for men as well as for women.

You don't expect loved ones to be as successful as you—you see yourself as the provider so they don't need to be—but you do expect them to give life their best shot. And it comes out in the way you ask them what they did today. Anyone with a long string of accomplishments gets a warm smile; anyone who complains about feeling bored or directionless receives a disapproving frown.

# AQUARIUS SUN/ARIES RISING

You have always been ahead of your time. And it's not because you're especially avant-garde or cutting edge. It's just that you can see further down the road than most and get impatient with the way people hold themselves back—worried about breaking rules or questioning commands. Clear-eyed and unsentimental, you put little stock in anything formulaic. You were made to upend, shake loose, and reimagine.

But you weren't always so radical. When you were young you were a good little soldier. Your Aries Rising ensured that you did what you were told and never stepped out of line. This won people's respect and trust and it still does. However, Aquarians were born with inventive minds, which means following the steps inevitably leads to mastering them. There comes a time when you see past the drill and start looking for ways to improve it. And as your confidence grows so does your willingness to march to the beat of a different drummer. There's nothing flippant about your Aquarian iconoclasm. It comes from a desire to remove the blinders and see things for what they are.

You're a truth teller—and like the truth, your bedside manner isn't always reassuring. Aquarians aren't very good at delivering bad news. They'll just present it matter-of-factly and push forward the box of tissues without skipping a beat. Thankfully your Aries Rising knows how to talk to people when they're down. That's because Aries is the sign of Coach Dad in Astrology. Yes, people need a minute to feel shitty about themselves but that's about as much time as you'll allow. What's important is to get them back on their feet. You'll start by commiserating about how they got a bum deal, then brainstorm about ways to make things better, and finally put together a plan to take back control from the situation that robbed them of it. No one knows how to embolden and empower like an Aquarius/Aries Rising.

You can lead, but not everyone will follow. Your ideas may be too far-fetched, your aims too bold, or your creative vision too ahead of its time. And this bestows a kind of loneliness. Nevertheless, your conviction is so resolute that you know people will catch up eventually and when they do they'll recognize how you were right all along.

## PISCES SUN/ARIES RISING

You put on a brave front. Your upper lip is so stiff and your gaze so steely that no one would ever imagine the depth of your feeling. And that's the point. Your Aries Rising knows there are two types of fish—shark and minnow—and that if you don't project a "don't mess with me" attitude then you're going to have a lot of hungry eyes checking out your tail. It's why you never let down your guard.

Suffering is built into your Sun Sign. Some say it's because you're sensitive and empathetic, but there's no escaping the fact that Pisces is the zodiac sign of sorrow. Maybe you experienced terrible loss when you were young, struggled with a childhood illness, or were abandoned by those who were supposed to look out for you. One would hope that you overcame your misfortunes heroically but it's never that simple. It's more likely that you experienced stumbles and falls, downward spirals, and self-destructive acts. You might even have been the source of others' pain. You understand the suffering and trauma that life all too often hands out.

Nothing cuts deeper than being called a "martyr." It's why you'll never say things are tough when they are or call attention to the sacrifices you make. Putting others' needs ahead of yours comes naturally and you don't ever want to be made to feel ashamed of it. Now it's true that there are those who make the world's suffering all about themselves, but you're not one of them. You're known for giving people the shirt off your back—and while you're at it maybe grabbing some extra shirts off other unsuspecting backs as well.

Unfortunately, that macho Aries Rising doesn't do you any favors by making light of your travails or changing the subject when the conversation gets too deep. This can be especially distancing with loved ones because it creates the impression that there are things you want to say, but won't. At first they'll push because they think you want to talk, but after a while they'll stop, which leaves you feeling lonelier than before. At some point you need to open up—for your sake as well as theirs.

# TAURUS RISING

You're comfortable in your own skin. You're pretty clear on who you are and don't pretend to be anything else. There's a "what you see is **You're comfortable in your own skin.** what you get" openness to Taurus Rising which immediately puts others at ease. Higher-ups don't feel like they have to worry about you and colleagues trust that you know what you're doing. You may start out at an entry-level position but you won't stay there for very long. Your reliability, consistency, and calm under pressure mean that you'll be shouldering major responsibilities and making the big judgment calls before long. You're the sort of person everyone asks themselves how they ever could have done without.

Your manner is gentle and kind. It's unexpected for someone who does the kind of regular heavy lifting that you do. Whether it's putting in the long hours or doing the grunt work, Taurus Risings are as strong as an ox. You'll keep going long after everyone else has caved in. Even if you have no chance of winning, you will still persevere to the end. This makes sense with the Taurus Risings who are built like a brick shithouse; however, it leaves people shaking their heads in disbelief when it shows up in Taurus Risings who are petite and demure. They still can't get over how physically powerful you are.

You clean up well. And it can be such a remarkable transformation that sometimes people don't even recognize you. Your preference is for comfortable clothes—pullovers and sweatpants that you can roll out of bed and into—but you can also glam it up if need be, and to spectacular effect. What else would one expect from a Rising Sign ruled by Venus, goddess of love and beauty?

The funny thing about Taurus Rising is how you can be sexy and *not* know it. Others assume it's false modesty or that you're playing games, but no, it's true. You really haven't a clue. You can have a bit of a paunch and still look dashing or wear just a touch of makeup and take people's breath away. It could even be argued that your innate nonchalance only adds to your charm.

And finally: the voice. It's why you never have to work that hard at capturing the interest of the most important person in the room. It might be throaty or melodic, seductive or soothing. Whatever its timbre it draws people near like a full-bodied wine. You could be reading aloud from the latest version of the tax code and people would still ask you not to stop. They never grow tired of listening.

# TAURUS SUN/TAURUS RISING

People start to make more money when you're around. And this isn't because you're a good luck charm or happen to possess the Midas touch. You just have a natural gift for growing things. Astrologers describe Taurus as practical and down to earth—mindlessly crunching numbers as if they were chewing cud—but there's more to your zodiac sign than that. Cattle were a sign of wealth in the ancient world—long before stocks and bonds. Indeed *cattle* and *chattel* both derive from the Medieval Latin word *capitale*, which is where we get the word *capitalism*. The root *caput* means "head"—and, as every rancher knows, *head* is the word you use for counting the number of cattle you own. "Bullish" is how Wall Streeters describe the market when the price of stocks is going up and "cash cow" is what we call any profitable venture that produces regularly and with little effort—like milking a dairy cow every morning. So you see, Taurus has been the symbol of wealth longer than money itself.

So does this mean you should turn in your acoustic guitar and become an accountant? Contrary to popular opinion, artistic pursuits and running a business aren't mutually exclusive. They don't occupy separate mental hemispheres. You can actually be both. Venus, the planet of love and money, rules Taurus, which means that it is possible to make a living doing something you enjoy. In fact, it's highly recommended.

Taurus/Taurus Risings often show up in the music industry because Venus rules song and dance. You'd make a great crooner or hoofer. But where other same-sign Sun Sign/Rising Sign combinations might focus only on their own performance, you know that you could use your brand to cultivate talent and produce up-and-coming artists. It's mistakenly assumed that anyone born under Taurus is content to be a beast of burden. You learned a long time ago that it's better to own than to rent. In other words, if you were to invest in the studio and sound equipment that others need to produce their music then you'll wind up making more than you would on your own. Venus is all about partnering because you get twice as much for half the effort. Work it right and you'll be enjoying passive income until the cows come home.

# GEMINI SUN/TAURUS RISING

You don't like surveys, have little use for feedback, and nothing annoys you more than unsolicited advice. As far as you're concerned, if something works—and it's successful—then it shouldn't be messed with. You abhor change for change's sake, but there's no denying that that's the world we live in. That's why you will sit there smiling and nodding in all the right places while supervisors share their suggestions, analyses, and work-shopped ideas on how to improve things. You know that expressing resistance would only send up a red flag—earmarking you for more tedious "conversations"—while playing along signals that you're on board with the program. Afterward, when people have lost interest in their pet causes, you can always change things back to the way they were before. When you're a Gemini/Taurus Rising, blending in with the rest of the herd is the best way to get to where you want to go.

You're very good at playing the game. It's something Geminis excel at. Knowing that you get more flies with honey than you do with vinegar makes you an expert flatterer. You never argue and you're never brusque. People are your means to an end, which is why you put a lot of time and effort into cultivating relationships. You're like a grocer constantly checking the produce to make sure it's fresh. You remember everyone's name, reply immediately when texted, and are always ready with a fun fact or newsie item to break the ice. Is it any wonder that you're the one sent in to interview a prospective hire or placate an upset client? Your people skills are unrivaled.

Ironically the perfect environment for you is one with a lot of hustle and bustle. One wouldn't know it to look at you. Your wardrobe is so uniform that one would swear you had closets full of the same identical clothes. Actually it's subtle variations on a theme, but you're not telling. Nevertheless it's this very stability you bring to situations in danger of veering off course that makes you invaluable. What's also extraordinary is your ear for music. You can tell when the pitch is off or a note falls flat. Chances are you taught yourself how to play an instrument. This talent allows you to tune in to whomever you're speaking to.

# CANCER SUN/TAURUS RISING

Small things are safe with you. Whether it's a fumbling infant, a sprouting seed, or the barest traces of an idea, you will nurture, cradle, and protect it. You understand that life is different in its early stages. It has to be handled delicately. It requires your full attention and can't be hurried. Many people want a guarantee before they sign on for any kind of commitment. They don't want to waste time or lose money. But life doesn't work like that. You have an innate understanding that you can't ask for the result without putting in the work. It's why you give of yourself so completely knowing that things could take a disappointing turn without warning. Nevertheless you have to be brave enough to try and patient enough to care about how it all turns out.

You were born during the time of day when it's still night outside, so your Ruling Planet—the Moon—is powerful. This makes you more instinctual than intellectual. You're always checking in with your gut to see what the next move should be—even if you work as a biochemist. The uptick in lunar energy also bestows an innate ability to find your way in the dark. Never quick or sudden, you approach things slowly and deliberately—trusting in a process that you're not all that sure about. This can be maddening for people who want you to do things their way; rewarding for those wise enough to let you do that thing that you do. You know that digging up a seed every other day to see how far it's come isn't the way to grow a flower. You have to let nature take its course.

Cancer/Taurus Risings are extremely tactile. Taste, touch, and smell are your strongest senses. That's why you're always picking up things to sniff, squeeze, or sample. It's very foodie of you and indeed many Cancer/Taurus Risings make great chefs, gourmets, and sommeliers, but it can get a bit much when you start opening up packages to see if you like what's inside and then putting them back on the shelf if you don't. You're the ones that present the empty can of soda or balled-up candy wrapper at the checkout counter because you couldn't wait. There's no such thing as delayed gratification with you.

# LEO SUN/TAURUS RISING

People pretty much do what you say. And it's not because you're loud or bossy. If anything, you're the opposite—cordial and understated. Yet you have this way of getting your point across that's unspoken but implicitly understood—almost as if you had leaned over and whispered something in the other person's ear. The result is a hurried nod and an open door where a closed one used to be.

You move around a place as if you owned it. And it doesn't matter if you're the one there for an interview. You could be facing a panel of stone-faced judges and within minutes they'll be asking you if you're comfortable or if they could get you something. When you're a Leo/Taurus Rising you don't enter a room looking for a job; you enter a room showing everyone how the job is done. This is more than just bluster or show. You've been around the block a few times and you know a thing or two.

Your Ruling Planet, the Sun, is at the lowest point of the horoscope when you're a Taurus Rising. This means you worked hard for everything you have. There were no lucky breaks, twists of fortune, or janitors teaching you chess in the school basement. You are completely self-made from head to toe because everything you've built is from the ground up. You leave nothing to chance or the imagination. You figured out your Coca-Cola formula early on and never go off script. You may not have great range and probably lack variety, but what you do have is consistency. Success isn't as flashy for Leos born at this time of day, but people would immediately notice that something wasn't right if you were gone.

Like any seasoned performer, you know your audience. It's why you only choose situations where people need you more than you need them. It's your way of being in charge. But this can get a little one-sided if you're not careful. That's why it's important to cultivate relationships outside your regular stomping ground. Taurus and Leo are two signs that can get fixed in their ways, so think about signing up for a class or doing volunteer work. Anything that gets you rubbing shoulders with people you wouldn't have met otherwise. It will open your world and replenish your soul.

# VIRGO SUN/TAURUS RISING

You're not afraid to talk money. You know your value and how much you should get paid. There is no negotiating, talk of commission, or coming down in price. Like Goldilocks testing out the mattresses to make sure she finds the one that's not too soft or too hard, you can intuit just the right amount to ask for. And you'll get it. If you don't? Then you know that working with or for this person would be a complete waste of time. Your number one rule is to never force a fit because you know from experience that it doesn't work. That goes for your professional *and* your personal relationships.

You benefit enormously from being a Taurus Rising. As a Virgo, you can't help but jump up and do whatever's asked of you posthaste. It comes from being born under the zodiac sign of work and service. Your Taurus Rising, however, is not in anyone else's hurry. Not only is it slow and methodical, it won't budge until it's been paid. This is a hard impulse for you to follow but you've seen that when you do, your salary goes up or the deal is made sweeter. Your bullish Ascendant isn't afraid to walk away from what's on the table if it isn't right. It won't try to make a situation work like your Sun Sign would.

The reason you strive to find the right fit with a client or customer is that you know your work is exceptional. Whether you're a forensic accountant, a glassblower, or a high-end consultant, you deliver top results. You will close yourself up in your office, burn the candle at both ends, and even sleep in your clothes for a week if that's what it takes to get the job done.

Your work is always concise and thorough and your attention to detail is so complete that you're itching to make tweaks to the product long after it's been turned in.

You're not thrifty. It's why people have a hard time believing that you're actually a Virgo. You're so free with the food and wine—especially when you're celebrating your success. However, there's no mistaking your Taurus Rising when you start boasting about how much the meal cost—and then pass around the check for everyone to see.

# LIBRA SUN/TAURUS RISING

People have no idea what it took to get to where you are today. The years spent improving your circumstances, refining your taste, and polishing your look. To say that you started off as a diamond in the rough would be an exaggeration. Used to being overlooked early in life, you shouldered the burdens and dutifully did what you were told. You didn't think twice about stepping aside to make way for more privileged personalities—like a favored sibling or a spoiled cousin—to pursue opportunities that were deemed theirs. You might have even helped fund them.

Then came the chance discovery. The fairy godmother friend who saw in you something nobody else saw. Maybe it was a teacher, a mentor, or the popular girl who decided to take you on as a pet project. They prevailed upon you to level up your grooming and styling game. These may sound like cosmetic changes, but cosmetic changes pack the power of a religious conversion when Venus rules both your Sun Sign and Rising Sign. They show you a picture of what you could be and then it's up to you to make that image a reality. Once you commit to that, everything in your life changes and you go from the person behind the curtain to the one wowing the audience.

Some might say you're trying to pass as something you're not, and comments like that cut deep. They reveal the guilty secret that you're not really the person you present yourself to be. Now one could say: Who is? And they would be right. But this is something that's often experienced in astrological charts in which the Sun is as far away from the Ascendant as yours is. There's a wide divide between the face you show the world and who you are underneath. Sometimes it can make you feel inauthentic.

Artists study artists like athletes study athletes. They don't mimic them, but rather look for the things they can absorb and turn into their own. All of this is aimed at improving your signature performance. Taking what someone else does and making it better is something that Libra/Taurus Risings excel at. And you should never feel indebted to the people you borrowed from. If anything, they should feel indebted to you.

## SCORPIO SUN/TAURUS RISING

It looks like life has been good to you. You have everything one could ask for—a prestigious career, a successful partner, a loving family, and the sort of luxurious home that only appears in Ralph Lauren ads. It's a life that could easily be mistaken for a photo shoot. And it's because things are so picture perfect that you're careful not to imply that it might be otherwise. Nothing in life is free. Everything comes with a price. And when you're a

Scorpio Sun with Taurus Rising, you never let on about how expensive the upkeep can be.

Scorpio is a tortured soul. There's no way of getting around it. A strong believer in the more you have the more you stand to lose, you guard what's yours vigilantly. You savor every moment and drink in every intimacy because you know that anything you love is a hostage of time. There are people who move about the world freely with ease and grace—ignorant that what's theirs today could be gone tomorrow. You wish you could live in that state of denial. Yours is a never-ending anxiety; a constant worry about being hurt, left, or cheated. But nobody ever sees this side of you because you won't let them. The only giveaway is when you hug a little too long or abruptly bring the conversation to a close.

Taurus and Scorpio are all about security. For Taurus it's financial, and for Scorpio it's emotional. Emotional security is harder to shore up because feelings change. One day they're safe and secure and the next they're gone—the vault emptied out by a loss of interest or because somebody else came along. Something that Scorpio Sun/Taurus Risings have to watch out for is using money to keep people on a short leash. Your Rising Sign has a natural sense of ownership whenever it spends money on someone. Mix in that famous Scorpio fear of abandonment and the possessiveness can get stifling. One of the hardest things to learn is the tighter you squeeze, the more the other person will want to slip away. You need to let go in the moments when you're most afraid of losing someone. It sounds counterintuitive, but you'd be amazed by how well it works.

# SAGITTARIUS SUN/TAURUS RISING

Life should be lived to its fullest. That's your philosophy in a nutshell. Actually, it's more like a mandate. People talk about their bucket lists—you know, those things they want to do before they die? Well, yours is a list of things you want to do before the end of the month. You don't believe in postponing anything when it comes to fun and pleasure. You've watched too many sad souls never get around to doing the things they said they were going to do one day, and you won't be one of them. When you leave this planet it will be with every penny spent, sight seen, and moment experienced.

People are in for a surprise if they think you're going to follow the nine-to-five routine. You're a Sagittarius, and centaurs have an insatiable thirst for adventure. Convinced that the best things in life are happening someplace else, you don't think twice about booking the next flight out. And if anyone asks you where you're going, your answer is: "Anywhere but here."

Now this sounds like it would fly in the face of your bovine Ascendant. Taurus Risings are supposed to be staid, domestic, and stay at home. But anyone who's been around bulls and horses knows that these two animals don't take kindly to being ridden by just anyone. Ask any rodeo cowboy. They have a wild side and will buck, rear, and spin to throw off anything unwanted. Those who assume that you'll just peacefully graze in any old pasture are in for a rude awakening. Your Sun Sign doesn't take a back seat to your Ascendant. That would be like putting the cart before the horse.

You're the eligible single everyone asks questions about. How come you're never home? Why aren't you married? Don't you want to have kids?

The truth is you don't want to be saddled with a thankless obligation. You've gone out with too many free-spirited types only to discover that they were really like animal rescues searching for a home. And as for children? Having a family isn't exactly a burning priority—you're surrounded by fascinating people of all backgrounds and ages—but should you decide to, it would be in your own way and in your own time.

# CAPRICORN SUN/TAURUS RISING

People always knew you'd be something one day. You clearly had the talent and the smarts. That was obvious from day one. It's just that they—as well as you—never fully understood how long it would take. Capricorn is ruled by Saturn, the planet of time. That explains why things take twice as long to come together for you and take twice as long to fall apart. And this isn't based on you being cautious or methodical. It really is a timing issue. You just happen to live and work at a slower pace than most people. Add to this that Saturn is also the planet of detours and delays and you can see why you spent so many years traveling long and winding roads, heading down blind allies only to be forced to go back the way you came, or standing atop one pinnacle of achievement only to find yourself longing for another. They say that Capricorn is the most ambitious sign of the zodiac and that's true. But nobody ever said that you were going to be quick about it.

Luckily your Taurus Rising ensures that you never do without. If you're going to scale those heights then you'll be doing it with the best friends, the latest gear, and a knapsack full of food and drink. Taurus is an earth sign—just like Capricorn—which means that you have to take care of your body if you plan on going the distance. No spartan stoicism or self-destructive angst for you. You don't want to burn out or go into a nosedive right when you're on the verge of getting what you want.

Perhaps the most telling realization is that you're not fated for one stupendous breakthrough or blazing triumph. Rather your success comes in dribs and drabs—like an allowance parceled out by the Stars. You get just enough to keep on going, but not so much that you stop working. And then one day you wake up to discover that people in your field now regard you as an elder statesman, someone to revere and consult. But the funny thing is you don't remember having made it. Success for a Capricorn/Taurus Rising is always cumulative—which explains how you missed out on crossing the finish line in the first place.

# AQUARIUS SUN/TAURUS RISING

You're always surprised when people are startled by something you propose. You could be walking them through a budget, solution, or game plan and they will all still have the same reaction: How did you come up with that? Turning ideas on their heads and familiar routines inside out is something you do naturally—like a gymnast going through their floor exercises. But what leaves everyone astonished is how perfectly obvious it all is once you explain it. What was a complete muddle moments before now makes absolute sense.

You're a structural thinker. That's something Taurus and Aquarius have in common. But where Taurus is practical, Aquarius is abstract. Think of it as a footpath. Taurus lays the stones and Aquarius measures the space between them. Together they create something that's both useful and beautiful to look at. This is why so many Aquarius/Taurus Risings go into landscaping, design, and architecture. You have this uncanny ability to connect the dots and reveal a figure where random markings used to be.

But you are also equal parts predictable and unpredictable—especially when it comes to your emotions. One moment you can be warm and snuggly and the next you're cold and distant. That's why intimates are always asking what's wrong or if they said anything to offend you. They're not used to feelings being turned on and off so casually. That's why you have to make more of an effort to read *their* emotional signals. It may feel like you're learning a foreign language at times, but it's something that mutual friends and relatives can help out with.

The beauty of having a Taurus Ascendant is that it grounds you. It puts you in a body in space. It allows you to be here now instead of projecting into the future. You need this because Aquarius Suns tend to live in their heads. It also attracts people into your life who are comfortable with getting naked. You may start out as the world's most paint-by-numbers lover, but you'll get the hang of it in time. In fact the more you practice, the more you'll come to enjoy it. Your Taurus Rising also gives you a love of food, wine, and luxury. It provides a curvaceous shape to a Sun Sign that tends to be too austere and streamlined.

# PISCES SUN/TAURUS RISING

The right person always seems to come along at the right time. Maybe it was the kid at school who introduced you to their family that felt more like family than the one you were raised in, the foreign lover who showed you what life looks like on the other side of the world, or the mentor who took you under their wing and taught you how to soar. Some of these encounters are fly-by-night, in town to help turn your life around before jetting off again, and some of them go on to become mainstays. But whatever their rank, they have each contributed to you being you—like a stream pouring into a river. You are the sum of each and every one of them.

Things happen to you more than you happen to things when you're a Pisces/Taurus Rising. It's something you're not very proud of. You're often criticized for going with the flow or being led around by the nose. And you've certainly had more than your fair share of experiences where you've been duped, deceived, and ill-used. Yet what's impossible for people to understand is how this has a funny way of turning out well in the end. Not only because the people who treated you badly always wind up getting their comeuppance—often contacting you years later to beg your forgiveness—but these experiences also enrich you emotionally, spiritually, and even financially. It's amazing how many Pisces/Taurus Risings end up in strangers' wills or listed as a beneficiary without even knowing it.

The Pisces Sun makes you creative, but it's the Taurus Rising that makes you productive. Without that earthy Ascendant, you would just fantasize about all the things that you could do if only circumstances were more conducive. It's your Rising Sign that gets you to roll up your sleeves and put your shoulder to the wheel.

The only things that you do have to keep tabs on are your physical cravings. You're always hungry, thirsty, or horny. When your Rising Sign is ruled by Venus—named after the goddess of love—and your Sun Sign is ruled by Jupiter and Neptune—two Roman gods famous for not keeping it in their togas—then let's just say you never met a bacchanalia you could say no to.

# ARIES SUN/TAURUS RISING

People know better than to get on the wrong side of you. And it's not because you're temperamental, vengeful, or will make a scene if you don't get what you want. It's that you will mow down anyone who gets in your way. Standing up to you when you have your mind set on something would be like standing up to a stampeding herd of cattle. It's just not a good idea.

There's a confidence that comes with being the biggest person in the room. People step out of the way, nobody encroaches on your turf, and you always get noticed by the bartender. But remember that not all Taurus Risings are physically large—in fact, some Aries/Taurus Risings are quite the opposite—but you still carry this feeling of largeness around with you. It's a good thing to have because people won't mess with you, but little do they suspect that you're really a gentle giant underneath.

The downside is when you get fixated on making yourself smaller. You may think you're too heavy, too tall, or that you take up too much space. You may see yourself as ungainly no matter how much loved ones and friends say otherwise. And this is more than just a self-image problem. It reflects the disconnect between the Aries Sun—which wants to be a lean, mean fighting machine—and the Taurus Rising—which likes to stop and smell the roses, and maybe even grab a bite to eat while you're at it. Hopefully you're comfortable with yourself because if you are then life is good. If not? Then you can attract people who put you down, criticize your appearance, and prod you into becoming a lesser version of yourself. The danger with having a Rising Sign next to your Sun Sign is that it creates a blind spot that makes you prey to those who are only too happy to take advantage of it.

You may have to go through a few relationships or working situations where you hand your power over to someone who doesn't deserve it before you realize that it's good to be the bigger person. Small-mindedness cramps your style. And once you see that it's better to be a Gulliver than a Lilliputian, you'll snap free of your constraints and never sell yourself short again.

# GEMINI RISING

♊

You don't address people face-to-face, but rather shoulder to shoulder. Maybe it's the sideways glance, a knowing chuckle, or a muttered remark **You like to keep people guessing.** that was meant to be overheard. This is how you test the intelligence of a potential acquaintance. Did they pick up on your innuendo or did it go right over their head? Most of us try to get a read on someone by searching their eyes or deciphering their demeanor. You decide if they're in or out based on how they play. If someone's quick with a comeback, they're in. If they're slow and lumbering: out. Unless they're cute. And even then you don't expect things to last for very long.

You have an incredibly active face. It refuses to sit still. Expressions race across it like schoolchildren let out of class at the end of the day. It's always busy frolicking, jostling, espying, or scowling in disagreement. One moment it's listening excitedly to what someone has to say and then the next it's leaning in closer with conspiratorial interest. Anyone can read your thoughts. You broadcast them for the entire world to see. The problem is that they all fly by so fast that it's hard to be sure if that was you in the moment or you for real.

You like to keep people guessing. And it's not because you're trying to be unpredictable or mysterious. It's because you are constantly making

**Nobody works a room better than a Gemini Rising.** up—and unmaking up—your mind. You're like an artist doing multiple sketches before putting paintbrush to canvas. Thickening a line here or adjusting a limb there as you work to get the image right. That's why you're always throwing out ideas, questions, and hypothetical scenarios haphazardly. None of these are supposed to be taken seriously. They're hardly your final draft. It's just you thinking out loud and taking the pulse of the room while you're at it.

Nobody works a room better than a Gemini Rising. You're naturally curious about people and their opinions of *other* people. Ruled by Mercury, the messenger of the gods, Geminis are good at communicating, but there's more to Mercury than witty repartee or a clever turn of phrase. The only deity able to travel from heaven to earth to hell and back again, Mercury was Jupiter's eyes and ears in Roman mythology. Jupiter knew people were always on their best behavior at religious rituals, so it was Mercury's job to report on what was *really* going on behind those prayers and incantations. This is why you're the information gatherer, the one everyone turns to for the latest scoop or juicy details.

## GEMINI SUN/GEMINI RISING

You're everyone's favorite rascal—always hatching a plan or concocting a scheme to escape some oppressively dull and dreary situation. A familiar face in after-school detention, your track record of mischievous behavior and unexplained absences continues to this day in the workplace. One would think you'd be deemed unhirable by now except for the fact that supervisors find you irresistibly charming. They want to be the ones to develop your potential and turn you into a productive member of the company. They might even see you as their personal project. And for those who are onto your shenanigans? They know how smart you *really* are, which is why they want you on their side working for them rather than against.

There's no shortage of wiliness when you're a Gemini/Gemini Rising. Not only can you outsmart and outtalk the competition, but you're also gifted with your hands. Indeed your Ruling Planet Mercury rules over eye-to-hand coordination. This allows you to type, program, and input at the speed of thought. Formidable skills should you ever want to make a career of gaming. It also allows you to excel in illustration, design, and packaging. You have a sixth sense for what catches people's interest and can transform a tired concept into something smart and stylish.

But you bore easily. It's why you bounce from job to job or relationship to relationship. This is what creates the impression that you're bright but superficial. Now this would be fine if you really were shallow; however, the problem with a quick mind is that it assumes it knows everything at first glance. Convenience trumps concentrated effort so that over time you wind up lowering your sights and narrowing your horizons. It's important to take on challenges that stump you or endeavors that require more than an afternoon of your time. It exercises your brain and deepens your thought process.

Gemini/Gemini Risings are only as good as the crowd they hang out with. Born under the sign of the twins, it makes perfect sense that you would duplicate the mannerisms of a close friend or sibling. You might even start to dress alike. This is good if this person's a positive influence, but not so great if they aren't. That's why you can never be too picky about whom you hang out with.

# CANCER SUN/GEMINI RISING

People never see you coming. And you like it that way. When you target something you want—whether it's a person, job, or prized object—you will retreat rather than approach. You need time to scope out the terrain, familiarize yourself with the story, and check to see if you know anyone who can move you closer to what you're after. Everything you do is strategic. You never act on impulse. Reaching out and grabbing something could end up in your hand getting slapped, while gently inserting yourself into the action wins trust and acceptance.

You're naturally chummy. Your Gemini Rising is an expert at small talk and can find something curious and fascinating in the most humdrum conversations. Indeed it's that gift of gab that wins people over. You can hobnob with narcissists as easily as you commiserate with curmudgeons. No one ever thinks of you as working an angle because you come across as genuinely interested and thanks to your Cancer Sun, you can make complete strangers feel like you've been friends for years. You're the person everybody loves, but nobody ever really knows.

You always get what you came for, but never call attention to it. You never trumpet your accomplishments or gloat about your victories. That would only make people feel duped. As softly as you worked your way into their lives, you will just as imperceptibly extract yourself from their lives. It may be months before they even realize that you're gone.

As you can imagine, a Cancer/Gemini Rising would make an excellent con artist or thief. Thank heavens you pop up in more benign professions like buyers, collectors, and investors. It's true you have a hidden agenda, but the nice thing about you is that you have the good sense to keep it hidden. The only place where you might run into trouble is with intimate relationships. Not everyone gets this double life of yours. The smart ones, however, can tell when they're being played and will even match you move for move. This explains why you often end up in bed with the competition. Obviously there's a sleeping-with-the-enemy thrill, but should you successfully find a way for your interests to dovetail then this can become a long-term thing. The fact that you will always keep each other guessing is the secret to your relationship.

## LEO SUN/GEMINI RISING

You know you're pretty special and that you make an enormous difference in people's lives. You bring the show. It's your name that sells tickets, your presence that creates excitement, and your stamp of approval that greenlights a project that would have loitered forever in limbo. No other zodiac sign places such a high value on individuality as Leo does. The Leos of the world keep everyone from disappearing into the woodwork of consensus. You insist on integrity, accountability, and being true to yourself.

Self-confidence is great, but it can also be perceived as overbearing if it isn't kept in check. This is why Leos can be seen as egotistical and self-serving. However if you're a Leo with Gemini Rising then you have an innate ability to put people at ease. You were born with a twinkle in your eye and a sly smile that says that no matter how grown up you appear on the outside, you're still a child at heart on the inside. And this is something others see right away. You have no problem walking up to total strangers and starting a conversation. You can read body language like an impersonator and can quickly size up someone's qualities. It's crazy how you can intuit just the fun fact, quirky story, or play on words that puts people at ease and gets them to chuckle and open up about themselves. You're the person everyone wishes they had become best friends with on their first day of kindergarten. If they had then they might never have felt so judged or rejected.

When you're a Leo with Gemini Rising, you can see what makes each person special and you will encourage that person to shine in his or her own unique way. They don't have to be the best at what they do, they just have to be fabulous when they do it. You're really good at getting others to stop trying to be something they're not and to just commit to being themselves. This is why Leo/Gemini Risings make such great teachers, coaches, mentors, and talent scouts. You know how to bring out the best in people. And like anyone fortunate enough to have an air sign Ascendant, the more you bring out the best in others, the more they bring out the best in you.

# VIRGO SUN/GEMINI RISING

You still get carded at thirty. People say it's a nice problem to have, but being mistaken for younger has its downside. Everyone talks down to you, refers to you as "cute," and is genuinely surprised when you come up with a solution that might actually work. You've often wondered if you haven't been passed over for positions of authority because your boss is afraid no one will take you seriously or a client just doesn't see you as being up to the job. It's something that rankles you, but when you try to talk about it to people they just pat you on the head and make a sad boo-boo face.

So what's wrong with letting people believe what they want to believe? Just because they think you're naïve and innocent doesn't mean you are. If anything, you can use their assumptions to your advantage. Gemini and Virgo are both Mercury-ruled signs, which means that you're very good at games. Gemini's wiliness comes from its love of play. It literally makes things up as it goes along, which is why it's so adept at improvising on the spot. If anyone can pull a rabbit out of the hat last minute—it's your Rising Sign.

Virgo's smarts come from watching and learning. It's an accrued knowledge based on studying what people did right and more important: analyzing what they did wrong. Your challenge is to work out of both headspaces. Follow your Gemini Rising's impulse to wing it and let your Virgo Sun's genius for detail make the necessary adjustments along the way. This allows you to refine, perfect, and, in some cases, salvage. Virgos figure out how to make a situation work best by tinkering. It's your hands-on method of discovery. And while you're at it you could also benefit from your Rising Sign's penchant for bending the rules. That Virgoan insistence on lining everything up correctly often hobbles your more creative leaps.

You're never going to get anywhere feeling like you have to prove yourself. That's playing by other people's rules, not yours. Once you make the shift in thinking from precocious to practiced, you'll see that you're the one who's steering the situation and that everyone else is simply following your lead. This moves you from the child's seat to the place behind the wheel.

# LIBRA SUN/GEMINI RISING

You have this lovely way of putting others at ease. And it doesn't matter if you're addressing an anxious CEO or a panicked child lost in the parking lot, everyone knows that they're in good hands with you. One could say that it's your grace under pressure that wins them over, but what it really comes down to is your reassuring tone. There's something about its timbre that conveys the feeling that everything is going to work out. And the reason people believe you is because it usually does.

No one knows how you produced that solution out of midair. Things can be in utter chaos one moment and then suddenly there's the folder of deleted files, the name of the expert who can help, or the relieved parents exhausted with worry. Reuniting lost objects with their keepers and restoring good faith among broken ties are things that come naturally. When you're a Libra/Gemini Rising, not only are you resolved to make things right again but you also have the means to do it.

Nevertheless, Gemini Risings have a mischievous side. This is the part of you that secretly inspects your dinner host's medicine cabinet or presses the "do not press" button when nobody's looking. Some of you have even been known to slip an unpurchased item into your purse or pocket. Obviously this goes against everything your Libra Sun believes in, but there's no denying the thrill that comes with getting away with something you shouldn't be doing. It's your little reward for always being good.

One of your biggest problems is talking yourself out of something you know is right. Second-guessing is a chronic air sign debility, but it becomes heightened with Gemini Rising. Not only does this mercurial Ascendant exacerbate Libra's famous indecisiveness, it can also lead you to play one confidant against another as you search for the correct answer—which is usually the one you started out with. Try limiting yourself to three "What do you think?"s in a meeting. Any more than that and you're just going around in circles.

You're always rushing into relationships. Thankfully Gemini is the escape artist of the zodiac and has a sixth sense for emergency exits and loopholes. This allows you to disentangle yourself from all the dry runs until you hit upon the person who's right for you.

# SCORPIO SUN/GEMINI RISING

It's not easy having a split personality. Those who don't know you very well see someone who's outgoing, chatty, and all kinds of naughty fun. They admire your sharp turn of phrase and giggle at your double entendres. Fond of satire, you have this ability to push a jest to the limit without ever crossing the line between clever and mean-spirited. Indeed, most everyone would be hard pressed to think of someone who's smarter, faster, and slicker than you. You're not the sort that anyone would want to match wits with, yet little do they suspect that behind this lighthearted comedian lies a sulking, skulking Scorpio.

Sometimes it feels like you're the dirty secret when you're a Scorpio with Gemini Rising. You take everything seriously, wound easily when rejected, and harbor grudges like a barfly nursing a last-call cocktail. Romantic interests quickly find out that you're not what you advertised. You're much more insecure and defensive. One would think you were two entirely separate people, but you're not. The Gemini Rising is not some mask that you put on. It's as much a part of you as the Scorpio is.

Gemini Risings are often cast in the role of the go-between. Ruled by Mercury, named after the fleet-footed god of messages, you have an intrinsic familiarity with all the ins and outs and are adept at navigating any tricky terrain. Combined with Scorpio's natural ability to face facts no matter how grim, you're the one who's asked to break the bad news, dig up the dirt, or put the final nail in the coffin. Scorpio/Gemini Risings are natural muckrakers, but you can just as easily work for the other side too. Some might regard you as an opportunist because of your love of money but you have your own way of ensuring that justice is served. If anyone can expose the wolf in sheep's clothing while revealing the sullied past of the innocent lamb—it's you. Moreover, you will make them both confess and do penance.

You may feel at times like you're too messed up for anyone to love, but people are a lot more caring and clever than you take them for. You won't meet many, but when you find them, do yourself a favor by opening up and cherishing them in your life.

# SAGITTARIUS SUN/GEMINI RISING

You know the most fascinating people. No unholy boors or pale wallflowers cling to you. You make a point of avoiding downers and losers and only hang out with larger-than-life personalities who are outstanding, brilliant, and going places. It's extraordinary to think about whom you knew when and the pivotal role you played in their lives. Why, to hear you tell it, you're the one who first encouraged Meghan to go on that date with Harry, tried to warn Kim that Kanye was trouble, and told Dr. Jill Biden about this kid named Amanda who's really good at poetry.

Friends gave up on fact-checking you a long time ago. Those tales are so tall and the coincidences so incredible that the real fun isn't in debunking them; it's in seeing what you'll come up with next. And you don't disappoint. You have an audacious imagination. But the strange thing is there's always an element of truth to what you say. Maybe it really was an old friend of yours that was buddies with Meghan in the fifth grade or a client you do business with who used to party with Kanye. A little snip here or an embellished detail there doesn't detract from the possibility that you *could* have met. It's not completely out of the question. As far as you're concerned, six degrees of separation is the next best thing to being there.

Putting a positive spin on things is something Gemini Risings do best. It's why you often pop up in sales, marketing, or publicity. You have an uncanny instinct for what the public wants. This along with the unembarrassed gushing that all Sagittarius Suns possess is what gets people to leave the line they're standing in to come join yours. Nobody can move product like you.

Booms, busts, and comebacks are all part of every Sagittarius/Gemini Rising's life cycle. Spouses may change and your appearance alter, but you're still the same person underneath despite all the rebranding and repackaging. People often wonder if you ever learn from your mistakes. Your answer to them is that making mistakes is integral to the creative process. You are the summation of your blunders and misadventures. The truth is something that was always meant to be stretched because nothing's duller than going through life just telling it like it is.

# CAPRICORN SUN/GEMINI RISING

Capricorns are famous for aging backward. You start out crotchety and grow more lighthearted with each passing decade. Add that sparkly Gemini Rising to the mix and it's impossible for anyone to determine how old you really are. You have a wise person's eyes, but a smart aleck's smirk. This is why people approach you cautiously. You look like someone they could like, but they're not too sure if you're all that likable underneath.

Most of this comes from your humor. It can be too acerbic for some tastes. Your ability to zero in on others' hypocrisies and to play them for laughs always gets the room going, but after the chuckles die down people can't help wondering what you might say about them when they're not around. And truth to tell, you wonder about that too. The typically taciturn Capricorn tends to get quite frolicsome when paired with this Mercury-ruled Ascendant and it's hard to tell if that's a relief or something to worry about.

There's a weird kind of serious-not-serious quality that's hard to pin down. One never knows when you're going to reveal something intimate or make a joke last minute. This stems from a pattern of deflect and test. Your Gemini Rising is a genius at getting others to look left when they should be looking right and your Capricorn Sun is always checking to see if someone is trustworthy or not. Indeed, those amusing conversations that loved ones and friends find delightfully entertaining are artfully designed to get them to show you their hand before you show them yours. You are always collecting information and assessing situations. One would think that you were a spy operating in enemy territory. And in a way you are because of your double life.

There's always a secret shame when you're a Capricorn/Gemini Rising. Maybe you came from the wrong side of the tracks, suffer from a condition you're afraid will ostracize you, or are atoning for some past sin. The easy solution would be to divulge everything, but the irony is that this secret shame motivates you to do all the wonderfully successful things you do. Remove that and you may lose your drive. The trick is to find a way to make peace with this private side of yours without letting it dominate your life altogether.

# AQUARIUS SUN/GEMINI RISING

You would do all the talking for both sides if someone let you. And it's not because you love the sound of your own voice or find silences awkward. It's just that you're so good at anticipating what the other party is going to say that you'll come out and say it. No apologies; no beating around the bush. Just you saying what's on the other person's mind. And the fact that you're so spot on can be unnerving for anyone who doesn't know you well. Indeed, going out with you is like dating a mentalist—which explains why so many potential love interests beg off after the first meet and greet. Some people have overactive imaginations whereas you have an overactive intellect. You accepted long ago that it takes a special kind of person to keep up with you, which is why you're rarely hurt when things don't work out. If anything, you're relieved.

You talk a lot. You talk when you're out with friends, you talk when you're by yourself, you talk in church and even in your sleep. You've been asked to leave many a yoga class because you can't help repeating what the instructor just said. Air signs narrate what they're doing all the time. It's their way of processing information. But most of them use their inner voice. When you're an Aquarius/Gemini Rising you can't help seeing all the possibilities to any given situation instantaneously and in your excitement to work out which ones are the most viable you'll often forget to press the mute button.

It's easy to mistake you for superficial. You're always on your phone and social interactions are swift and brief. But what appears to be a short attention span belies how quickly your mind works. Loved ones and friends know better than to ask you if you were paying attention because they know that you'll immediately recite what was said with the unerring accuracy of a court stenographer.

It's the Gemini Rising that makes you so personable. Without it you would sound didactic. Moreover, the newsie, conversational style of your Mercury-ruled Ascendant allows you to relate to people from all walks of life. It gives you your realness. Having your ear to the ground is helpful when you're born under a sign that often has its head in the clouds.

## PISCES SUN/GEMINI RISING

You are a deeply understanding and unusually sympathetic person. You know just the right questions to ask to make someone feel safe and like they can open up to you. You never force an issue or put words in anyone's mouth. An attentive listener, you can intuit which tangents to pursue and which to leave alone. Your gentle, coaxing manner is reminiscent of water lapping up against a boat. You can create this bubble of intimacy where people swear that you're talking only to them. Yours is the sort of voice one associates with a guided meditation, a therapist, or a poet; a voice that's easy to fall in love with sight unseen. That's why it's so disconcerting when you're overheard having nearly the same conversation with somebody else.

You have a lot of people to meet and greet. Life is like a revolving door when you have Gemini on the Ascendant. Now, you could treat everybody the same. It would make sense given the sheer volume of who you know, but a one-size-fits-all approach doesn't jibe with your one-on-one style. You really enjoy hearing everyone's stories and absorbing their histories and experiences. Nobody's as present as you. Yet there's such a demand on your time that you also have to handle them expediently. It's a balancing act. One doesn't expect a concierge to be personally invested in the welfare of each hotel guest, but they are expected to be courteous and to act like they care.

Your concern is not an act. Your Pisces Sun is so global in its outreach that it doesn't prioritize. Everyone is important to you. And this is why you're often accused of being fickle, fake, and misleading. People simply can't comprehend how you can replicate *their* special moment again and again. But that would be like asking the ocean to choose which beach it likes visiting most. Possessiveness is such a landmass thing and it simply doesn't translate to a Neptune-ruled sign like Pisces.

It's doubtful that you will ever placate jealous types so don't even try. Just send them on their way. Let's face it—you were born to be all things to all people, which means you need to be choosy about the company you keep. You will never be happy with anyone who makes you shrink to fit their expectations.

# ARIES SUN/GEMINI RISING

Things come quickly to you. It's almost as if you download information like a phone app. Others struggle to memorize or practice for hours, but you have such a natural facility that one or three tries may be all it takes. Now this doesn't mean that you're a genius. You don't automatically solve random math problems or speak any foreign language put in front of you. But if you're passionate about something then you will take to it like a champion to the contest and swiftly rise through the ranks to the top.

But just because things come easily doesn't mean you like it. You learned the hard way that you can be too talented for your own good. It's like being born beautiful. Everyone's smitten by what walks into the room but couldn't care less about the person underneath. As an Aries/Gemini Rising you're never sure which one people like most—your talent or you.

You can tell when someone's sizing you up. They might see you as a rising star—a protégé to be groomed and cultivated—or as a golden ticket out of a rut. You're used to people pinning their hopes on you. You were born during the time of day when the Sun is climbing to the highest point in the sky. You're bright and shiny, full of promise and potential. This makes you the sweetheart of coaches, mentors, patrons, and sponsors. They see in you the embodiment of their aspirations, and as an Aries you won't let them down. You will rise to the occasion of their expectations and—given your gumption and drive—surpass them. And you will repeat this throughout your life.

But what about the part of you that's not a performing machine? Being a Gemini Rising it's only natural to split your personality into public and private selves and to set them on parallel tracks so that they never intersect. This is OK if you're a hulking football player who likes to crochet in your downtime; it's not so OK if you present one way and then act out in another. You don't want those patrons cleaning up after your messes because they'll do whatever it takes to protect their investment. It's important to be you at all times—especially when it's competing with someone that others want you to be.

# TAURUS SUN/GEMINI RISING

You like to get chummy. You'll massage someone's shoulders, rest your leg against theirs, or skip the handshake and move right on in for a hug. This is your way of putting others at ease. Just like when you call them "honey," "dude," or some other nickname coined on the spot. Now this would be fine if you only did this with the people you know, but you'll also do it with just about anyone you meet. There's something both disarming and a tad invasive about your easygoing informality.

Taurus takes up space. It's why you'll sit with your legs spread out or throw your coat, scarf, and shopping bags onto the chair next to you without asking if it belongs to anyone. Add Gemini Rising to the mix and that's where the handsy quality comes in. You can't help touching people in all kinds of places. And it's not like you're trying to cop a feel; it's more like you're a grooming monkey. You don't think twice about flicking flecks of dandruff off their shoulder, straightening their tie, or pushing the hair up out of their eyes. At least you don't do what you normally do at home with loved ones, which is reach out and pop the pimple on their face without asking.

Obviously Taurus/Gemini Risings would make exceptional beauticians or cosmetologists, but you have a hungry intellectual side as well. You're eager to read all the talked-about books, to be fluent in the latest breaking news, and to stay current with upcoming fashions and cuisines. Venus and Mercury (the rulers of Taurus and Gemini) are naturally companionable. You can fraternize just as easily with the elite as you can with the person on the street. There are no limits to where you can go and loved ones and friends are often surprised to discover later who exactly you've been hanging out with.

Perhaps the most mysterious thing about Taurus/Gemini Risings is that nobody really has a clear idea of what you do for a living. Even if you own a business with your name on it there's always some sideline job or undisclosed revenue stream that you're involved with. You have a myriad of interests—some of them aboveboard and some of them under the table. You like to have a hand in a lot of different things.

# CANCER RISING

♋

You're more than happy to let someone else go first. Your thinking is if they're in that much of a hurry then they must really need to get to where they're going. Never one to obstruct or slow things down, you'll happily wait your turn. People often mistake this for passivity or even submissiveness, but they don't know how your mind works. You figured out a long time ago that those who make the first move don't always know what comes next. They rush out in front, but lack the means for staying there. Eventually they run out of steam or exhaust their resources—making them easy to overtake. Just because someone makes a big splash doesn't mean they know how to swim. You, on the other hand, are a keen observer. You study people, places, and things. You never make a move that's not premeditated and when you do act it's with the supreme confidence that you will achieve your goal effortlessly and without calling attention to yourself.

Cancer is ruled by the Moon, which is why most Cancer Risings have a Moon face—full, round, and glowing. There's a softness to your demeanor that appears rosy-cheeked and harmless. People aren't put off by you or threatened. If anything, they may be a little too quick to lower their guard. There's just something about you that feels homey, trustworthy, and familiar.

You rarely look someone in the eye for long. It's too confrontational.

**Cancer Risings never fight if they can help it.** Your gaze is downcast, to the side, or peers up coyly from a slightly tilted head. All of these things draw people closer. So does speaking quietly. Never one to raise your voice, you succeed at getting people to ask you what you're thinking rather than the other way around. You have a reputation for being someone who doesn't say anything unless there's something to say. And because your message is always one worth listening to, people refrain from interrupting and wait until you are finished.

Cancer Risings never fight if they can help it. You don't like the stress. But should you find yourself on the wrong end of an altercation, you won't cave in either. What you do is get boring. It's your version of playing dead in the animal kingdom. You have this ability to project a kind of psychic dullness. The utter lack of expression on your face combined with a penumbral pall saps the energy out of any hostile attack signaling to your opponent that they would be much happier rattling somebody else's cage. Once you know they're gone, you'll quickly pick yourself up and go about your day.

## CANCER SUN/CANCER RISING

Sometimes it feels like you live in an aquarium where all of your emotions are on display—like tropical fish swimming among the rocks and coral. Your darting affections and colorful fantasies; languid memories and pop-eyed anxieties. One would think you would be happy about this. Isn't being seen something we all crave nowadays? Maybe if you were a fire sign. Fire signs are expressive and want everything to be out in the open. Cancer is watery in nature, which means you value your privacy. You don't want people looking at you or tapping on the glass to try to get your attention. You want to be left alone and in peace.

This feeling of being on show is hard to escape. That's because there's no difference between the Ascendant and your Sun Sign. There's no role to play or persona to hide behind. You are you. It's especially stressful for a zodiac sign that wants nothing more than to blend in with its surroundings. Cancers are the hunters of the zodiac. It's why you absently hide your face with your hands or cover your traces with a manufactured story. Whether you're rummaging through the sales racks or have a love interest in your sights, you know you're not going to close in on your prey if you're being watched. Cancers pride themselves on their stealth. You want to slip in and out without anyone noticing you were there.

Your problem is you're better at hiding in plain sight than you think. Your assumption that everyone can read you like an open book makes you more secretive than you already are. Guarded about your word choices and careful to never give yourself away, you may be surprised to discover that you needn't have gone to all this trouble. People are so self-absorbed that you're lucky if they even look up from their smartphones.

Where all this surreptitiousness does the most harm is in your intimate relationships. You may assume loved ones know what's going on with you emotionally when they haven't a clue. And what's worse is that you won't believe them when they say so. It isn't easy for Cancer Sun/Cancer Risings to broach topics directly but the sooner you do, the sooner you'll clear up a lot of false assumptions and painful misunderstandings.

# LEO SUN/CANCER RISING

You exude warmth like a glowing hearth. People just want to come sit down next to you. Maybe they have something to say, maybe they don't; and that's OK because the silence never feels like anything that needs to be broken. It's restful. Somehow just being near you makes them feel sheltered and protected. They know that everything's going to work out—like in a bedtime story.

You've always had that parental vibe—even as a kid. Leo is a fatherly sign and Cancer is a motherly one so is it any wonder that you naturally take charge of situations and assume full responsibility? But you don't do it in a bossy way. You never override someone or cut them off. Your Cancer Rising is too subtle for that. You will patiently hear people out—letting them go on about their big plans, ambitious ideas, and how they're going to do things *their* way. And when they realize that they're out of their depth or have bitten off more than they can chew, then—and only then—will you step in. People are like children to you. You never want to quash their dreams, but at the same time you need to keep a watchful eye on how things unfold.

Family means a lot even though the one you came from wasn't exactly exemplary. One might say you're compensating by trying to get things right, but actually you're more focused on creating the family you always wanted. And that includes your lover or spouse who looks like they came from a background even more dysfunctional than yours. You believe in being in someone's corner; it's why you're so supportive and encouraging.

However, you also know that you can't be in someone's corner unless they're standing there themselves. This is something that you insist upon. You don't take on people who don't help themselves.

Money likes you and you like money. Part of it is your Midas touch, but mostly it's your eagerness to get in on the ground floor with a startup company or new business. You were born early in the day when the Sun was just starting out (it hadn't even risen yet) so you understand that it takes time for things to grow. It's this patience of yours that pays off over the years.

# VIRGO SUN/CANCER RISING

You won't do for someone, but you'll show them how to do it. It's the sort of thing that makes entitled bosses whine and needy co-workers yowl in hopes that you'll relent, but you won't. You're used to dealing with grown-ups' inner children. You've been dealing with them for years. It's why you can't be pushed around, guilt-tripped, or manipulated. You're impervious to being bought. What you will do, however, is start over from the beginning—for as many times as it takes—until the person you're teaching or training gets it right. You don't do things by rote or paint-by-number. Every life that comes into contact with yours is a life you feel responsible for and you will do your utmost to make your time together worthwhile and beneficial. You may not be in their lives for very long, but it's always for the right duration. Nobody ever forgets you.

It's amazing how quickly recalcitrant types fall into step behind you. And it's not because you have a take-charge personality or become scary when you raise your voice. You just have a way of doing things that strikes everyone as how they should have been done all along. Your philosophy is to break things down into three easy steps so that people can achieve their results quickly and efficiently. You also have a special talent for discerning how they absorb information. Not everyone learns in the same way. Some people are verbal whereas others are visual, aural, or need to sleep on it. By customizing your delivery you ensure that each person makes the information you impart their own. You are always encouraging them to find their voice, to draw on personal experience, and develop their own sensibility.

You may not be especially sentimental, but those who knew you when will certainly wax nostalgic about you. They remember you as the person who made complicated ideas accessible, who persisted when they wanted to give up, or taught them the value of a to-do list. The routines you established in their lives years ago are still followed today.

Loved ones have gotten used to sharing you with strangers. That's what happens when you're married to a beloved teacher. It's like being married to a celebrity. They understand that you belong to the world and they're OK with that.

# LIBRA SUN/CANCER RISING

You are highly sensitive to your surroundings. So much so that you will stop what you are doing to reposition a tilted picture or remove a dead flower from your orchid. Every piece of furniture is angled with fêng shui precision. The color on the walls needs to be soothing and the diffusion of light soft, balanced, and flattering. People should feel comfortable when they enter your space. You want them to be at ease but you don't want them to overstay their welcome, which is why you always glance at the clock whenever you sit down with someone to talk. You have a therapist's knack for telling when the time is up.

A lot of people listen, but you hear. You take in what others say and follow their stories through all the twists and turns. You can tell what's truthful and what was meant to throw you off the scent. However, the person you're listening to will never know what you really think. Both Libra and Cancer are famously nonconfrontational. There's no need to point out an inconsistency, press for information before someone's ready, or expose a lie. That will be done by somebody else. What you're there to do is assess— and that's best done by letting people believe that you are on their side.

Libra/Cancer Risings are excellent interviewers and mediators, which is why you often show up in HR departments. Your Libra Sun works very hard to remove any bias or prejudice. It's why you're assigned positions where it's up to you to render a judgment. Everyone trusts you'll be fair. And your Cancer Rising has an uncanny ability to make people feel relaxed. It's almost as if it emits negative ions—like an indoor fountain. If things don't work out with your HR career, you can always open a spa.

People often assume you have feelings for them when you don't. That's because you're naturally friendly and easygoing. Libra/Cancer Risings often avoid these awkward conversations by pretending not to notice but that's not good. The only thing worse than rejection is giving someone false hope. This is when you must nip this sort of attraction in the bud if it's not mutual. Yes, you're hurting someone in the moment, but it's better than allowing feelings to grow when you know you'll never feel the same.

# SCORPIO SUN/CANCER RISING

You hate it when the tears start welling up. It's embarrassing and happens when things get tense. This isn't how you picture yourself reacting in pressured situations. You want to be hard and cutthroat—the way that Scorpios are supposed to behave when they're under attack. Instead you can feel your lower lip quake and your voice crack. And even if you don't break down and cry, there will be some other wounded expression that broadcasts you've been deeply hurt. This gets people to soften their criticism and speak to you in gentler tones. It may be a sign of submission, but it's one hundred percent effective in getting the other party to back off. Your Scorpio Sun resents how your Cancer Rising just throws in the towel without even putting up a fight, but it's thanks to the Cancer Rising that you emerge with prize in hand or the goal within reach.

Scorpio is infernally proud. Ruled by Mars and Pluto, you'd rather die than give anyone the satisfaction of knowing they got the better of you. Moon-ruled Cancer, however, is not nearly so contemptuous. More into self-preservation than self-destruction, your Ascendant has no problem acquiescing, appeasing, or apologizing. It doesn't need to have the last word. Instead it's looking for a way to beat a discreet retreat so it can return and prevail another day.

Scorpio Sun/Cancer Risings are enormously creative. You love the arts and sciences and often succeed at both. Your obsession with unattainable objects drives your creativity. Whether it's drawing on past betrayals to write songs others listen to when they're feeling heartbroken or your stubborn refusal to let a problem beat you that prods you to go the extra mile—you will never give up. Everything you do comes from a personal place of pain and agony. This can get a bit tricky when something good comes into your life because there's always this fear that you will lose your edge.

The biggest thing for Scorpio/Cancer Risings to watch out for is the resentment that comes from having to apologize so much. You need to remember that you're the one who keeps on saying you're sorry so you can't get mad at people for accepting it because they're being polite. The vicious cycle ends once you stop apologizing for things so reflexively.

# SAGITTARIUS SUN/CANCER RISING

You can make yourself at home just about anywhere you go. Whether it's a penthouse duplex in Manhattan or a clay hut in Mali, you have no problem adapting to your surroundings. Sagittarius is a sign that's in love with the world and all the wonderful things in it. The delicate ecosystems of cultures, traditions, religions, and cuisines are like intoxicating ports of call offering you the chance to lose yourself in all their scents and colors. This is why so many of you will jump ship at the opportunity to study abroad or take jobs overseas without knowing a soul. Not only do you want to see the sights that can only be experienced in person, but you want to live the life you never could have lived had you stayed put. What starts off as a journey turns into a reunion when you discover your true home is nothing like the one you were raised in.

Now one would think that this would fly in the face of your Cancer Ascendant. Cancers are supposed to be homebodies who never travel further than their own backyards. Yet the Moon, Cancer's Ruler, was always seen as a wandering planet because it was never in the same place in the nighttime sky. It moved from one zodiac sign to the next practically every day. Moreover, the Moon was associated with Diana, goddess of the hunt. For centuries hunters followed game wherever it went—whether they tracked herds across long stretches of land or hunted whales halfway around the world. The Moon ruled the oceans long before Neptune was discovered.

But your wandering isn't just physical. It's spiritual too. Most people fascinated with a religion or belief system different from their upbringing will simply attend that house of worship. You need more. You will journey to its homeland repeatedly and, should the opportunity arise, settle there. Sagittarius/Cancer Risings are famous for going native.

And for those of you who aren't so willing to leave it all behind? You have a chameleon talent for picking up foreign languages, practicing others' customs, and mastering cuisines designed for different palates. Even the way you present yourself makes it hard for people to identify your background. Not that that matters. As far as you're concerned you truly are a citizen of the world.

# CAPRICORN SUN/CANCER RISING

Sometimes you can be a real cranky pants. Easily annoyed and unapologetic about it, you don't like it when people surprise you by adding an extra chore to the list or a request to their demands. There's nothing subtle about your sighs of exasperation. They're as loud as air escaping from a tire. Yet you will always do what's asked of you. Others may promise the Sun, the

Moon, or the Stars, but you deliver the entire nighttime sky. And it's this knowledge that you'll do whatever it takes to please a loved one that makes you even . . . crankier. Why? Because if anyone suspected how much you really cared about what they felt then they would exploit you shamelessly.

You don't want your heart to fall into the wrong hands, which is why you guard it as if it were the nuclear codes. Unfortunately, your Cancer Rising forms attachments to just about anything it lays eyes on. Whether it's a neglected antique in the back of a shop or an animal rescue staring at you beseechingly, your impulse is to take it home. You have your Capricorn Sun to thank for throwing cold water on some of your more misguided decisions. And even then there have been some close calls.

Camouflaging your feelings is exhausting. It would be so much easier if you could just turn them off—or better yet: not have any. You've met plenty of people who have the emotional depth of an inflatable pool. Why can't you be like them? Your Cancer Rising is as powerful as your Capricorn Sun—maybe even stronger—which means that neither zodiac sign is going to give an inch. Cancer is as true to its sentimentality as Capricorn is to its skepticism. Thankfully your lunar pull attracts people who can sense your internal struggle. They're the ones who make funny faces when you scowl, cheerfully wave away your complaints, and check in on you at the end of the day to make sure everything's all right.

You don't trust easily, which means that anyone who wants to get close to you has to give you plenty of time and space. It requires a lot of patience, but like the night-blooming Cereus, a cactus that only blooms a few nights a year, the wait is worth it.

# AQUARIUS SUN/CANCER RISING

You present as mild-mannered. Quiet, kind, and self-effacing, you've been putting other people's needs ahead of your own since you were a kid. Always quick to help out in a pinch or watch the dog while the owner is called away, you are the epitome of wholesomeness. If anyone could be described as the girl next door or the guy you can rely on, it's you. Yet Aquarius Suns with Cancer Rising are like superheroes with secret identities. Everyone accepts you at face value but hasn't a clue as to what you're really like underneath.

You tend to keep a tight lid on your ambitions. You don't want to upset the status quo. You realized a long time ago that you're smarter than most and better qualified, but to step out of line and show what you can do is asking for trouble. Not only do you risk being put on the spot and crumbling, but you may also find that you don't have the appetite for success you think you do. Your Cancer Rising has a strong need to belong. It doesn't want to rock the boat or cause any trouble. Unfortunately, Aquarius isn't one to look the other way. It's always being called upon to take the action everyone else is avoiding.

It's not easy being a lightning rod of controversy. It comes with being born under a zodiac sign that has a knack for being in the wrong place but at the right time for changing the course of events. You could be going about your day-to-day life, minding your own business when suddenly you're faced with a crisis. Maybe you accidently come across files that show your company is doing something shady or a friend swears you to secrecy about things that she shouldn't be silent about. Your Cancer Rising has the sort of face that people can trust with their secrets while your Aquarius Sun agonizes over whether keeping that secret is the right thing to do.

Doing what's right doesn't always feel right in the moment. Ask any whistleblower. However, Aquarius/Cancer Risings are farsighted enough to accept that what you're doing is for the best. Understandably friends and colleagues will have a hard time forgiving you, but you know that one day they will—and may even thank you for it.

# PISCES SUN/CANCER RISING

You are always around water. It doesn't matter if its spas, pools, lakes, or oceans, you are drawn to it like a Labrador retriever to a mud puddle. Anyone who knows you knows better than to interrupt you when you're taking a bath. This is your private time to slip beneath the bubbles and wash away the day's woes and worries. Some people find solace in quiet churches or spiritual retreats. You find yours communing with the element you were born in. Whether it's reminiscent of life in the uterus or your way of emptying out and opening up to the Collective Unconscious, you are restored and replenished by every splash or swallow. A water bottle is never far from reach.

Pisces is a dreamer. You have E-ZPass access to your imagination. Now everyone has a fantasy life, but few dive as deeply as you and resurface with something to show for it. Your imagination is a sunken treasure trove of ideas and images; forsaken myths and histories waiting to be refashioned into something original, timeless, and resonant. Pisces/Cancer Risings create the worlds that we visit in our novels, films, and video games. You can mesmerize like nobody's business.

Yours is a magical sign. One that people treat with awe and ambivalence. Awe because they're astonished by the wonderful things you come up with; ambivalence because you're not exactly dependable. Underwater time doesn't work like dry-land time. There are no dawns or dusks at the bottom of the sea. When Pisces goes to its underwater place, weeks and months can pass without them knowing it. And when they pop back up again—like one of those legendary kingdoms that materialize once every hundred years—they're as casual and chatty as if you had just gotten together for coffee yesterday.

Thankfully your Cancer Rising keeps you from wandering too far from home. The zodiac sign of family, your Ascendant keeps you firmly docked in the lives of loved ones and relatives. You may disappear into a daydream, but you're still physically present and accounted for. And this is the secret to your productivity. You may resent having bills to pay and mouths to feed, but it forces you to be productive instead of talking wistfully about all the things you'd like to do one day.

# ARIES SUN/CANCER RISING

You hate it when someone's upset. Cancer is the zodiac sign of the good mother, which means you will immediately stop what you're doing to see if this person's all right. And it doesn't matter if it's someone you abhor. Pain is pain and your impulse is to take them up into your arms and cradle them until they feel better. Obviously you can't do this in the middle of a business meeting, but you will make a point to touch base with the injured party afterward to make sure they're OK. Your Cancer Rising comes out whenever exchanges grow heated or the rough and tumble gets too rough.

As you can imagine, this doesn't exactly square with your Aries Sun. Aries is ruled by Mars, named after the Roman god of war. Nothing makes an Aries happier than to vanquish an enemy and revel in their defeat. Yet the curious thing about being an Aries Sun/Cancer Rising is that you are equal parts compassionate and combative. It's puzzling to those who don't know you well to see you egg on a friend to kick somebody's ass and then be the first one to help up the person whose ass has just been kicked.

The first medics were soldiers themselves. That's because in ancient times soldiers wounded in battle needed to be tended to by their comrades immediately or they would die, which meant that every soldier had to be familiar with cleaning and dressing a wound. It's a strange contradiction to think that every wounder was also a healer, but that's still true to this day. Your Ruling Planet Mars rules over knives and swords—weapons that cut; however, Mars also rules over the surgeon's scalpel—the instrument we rely on to delicately extract anything diseased or cancerous. Aries/Cancer Risings are just as likely to pop up working in ERs as they are in bustling restaurant kitchens.

Yours is the calm hand on the fevered brow, the commanding voice that forestalls the panic, or the chummy wink that reassures everyone that you're right there beside them. Never far from the action, you will push people to do the things they don't think they can. You will also help them to pick up the pieces when things fall apart. Your commitment to bringing out the best in others brings out the best in you.

# TAURUS SUN/CANCER RISING

Life looks better on a full stomach. It's amazing how you can magically produce a carton of ice cream from out of thin air or a bar of chocolate when there was nothing up your sleeve. And in times of heavy stress you've even been known to conjure up a perfectly tailored cocktail. You know that food is a great comforter, which is why you have it at the ready for heartbroken friends and demoralized loved ones. Taurus Sun/Cancer Risings are Astrology's great Rocks of Gibraltar—always there with a shoulder to lean on and a warm embrace. There's nothing craggy or weatherworn about you. If someone needs a place to stay until they can get their life back together then it will be in a well-appointed guest room with plump cushions and Egyptian cotton sheets. You're everyone's favorite shelter from the storm.

Indulgent and protective, you're not the best when it comes to letting people learn their own life lessons. You worry about whether they can handle the rude awakenings. This is why you avoid unpleasant conversations, dismiss incriminating facts, and would rather pay the bill than let anyone suffer the consequences of their mistake. You see it as looking after those closest to you, but it's a little more shadowy than that. Cancer is a mothering sign, and Taurus can be a possessive one. Cultivating dependence ensures that loved ones and friends never stray very far.

The result is that you can find yourself surrounded by people who never quite get their lives together. It's admirable that you want to shield them from the slings and arrows of outrageous fortune, but by doing so they wind up developing bad habits. Supporting people in avoiding hurdles doesn't help them to grow. If anything, it retards them.

The irony is you never relied on anyone to get to where you are today. You did it by yourself. Now if you truly want the people in your life to become what they were always meant to be then you need to get them out of the nest. And it doesn't matter if times are tough because if they don't learn to fend for themselves then they never will. It's OK to be there if they fall, but let them fall first. They may surprise you by pulling themselves out of their own nosedives.

# GEMINI SUN/CANCER RISING

People can't help feeling like they're not getting the whole story. There's something about the way you shift in your seat or avoid making eye contact that leads them to believe that you know more than you're letting on. And you do. It's Gemini's great contradiction to gain access to the most sensitive information but lack the ability to keep it to themselves. Given your druthers you'd dish the dirt and tell everyone everything you know but your Cancer Rising won't let you. Like a cosmic gag order, it's locked your lips and thrown away the key—leaving you to resort to cryptic remarks and darting glances.

When you were younger, you resented this feeling of being silenced by your own zodiacal censor. You never knew when it was going to shut down the conversation, but over time you've come to appreciate its timely intervention. More survival instinct than inner critic, you trust that it knows when to be still—like a fawn freezing in place because a predator is near. Your Cancer Rising has a sixth sense for danger—physical or emotional—and will instinctually avoid it. Your Gemini Sun, however, doesn't want to miss out. It can't resist pushing the boundary you were warned not to push.

When you're a Gemini/Cancer Rising you're often skating close to the edge. You may find yourself in questionable situations, involved in iffy transactions, or broaching uncomfortable topics. The amazing thing is how people who wouldn't respond to anyone else will respond positively to you. You always get the information you're looking for—and if it's unforthcoming, you have this uncanny gift for turning things into a guessing game where you keep asking if you're getting hotter or colder and the other person responds accordingly.

Where you get into trouble is when you don't pay attention to your crab antennae. Geminis have an unfortunate tendency to override their gut impulses with hypothetical what-ifs. And because the Sun Sign is stronger than the Ascendant, it will always win out. This explains all those decisions where you wished you had turned left rather than right. Thankfully you've survived and will continue to get yourself out of the corners you painted yourself into. Geminis are like cats—you have nine lives and you always land on your feet.

# LEO RISING

$\mathcal{\Omega}$

You possess a noble bearing. And it doesn't matter if you were born on the wrong side of the tracks or without a penny to your name; you strike people as destined for greatness. You radiate success and everyone can tell that you're going places. That's why doors open, opportunities beckon, and gifts are laid at your feet. You don't go looking for good fortune; good fortune comes looking for you. Now it might seem odd that the first impression you make carries such an enormous impact—you're surprised by it yourself—but that's what happens when your Rising Sign is ruled by the Sun. It's like having a gold star next to your name. And if that's the way others are going to treat you, then why argue?

Now it isn't always easy to tell if people want the best for you. On one hand, you're keenly aware of their fondness for you. They make no secret of their admiration—praising you for all the things that you do and going on and on about how wonderful it must be to be you. And with your Leo Ascendant you can't help responding like a purring kitten. Flattery will always be your weakness. Yet it's hard to shake this feeling that you're also being set up for failure. Are you really as good as they say? And what happens if you're not? You're surrounded by great expectations and the unspoken rule that you live up to them.

Leo Risings are often described as arrogant. And there's some truth to that because when you live out in the open like you do, you must be bold. You learned a long time ago that it's better to take command of a situation than allow it to take command of you. You may not know what you're doing half the time, but if anyone can fake it until they make it, it's a Leo Rising. Your supreme confidence that everything will work out for the best projects conviction. It's amazing how quickly people fall into line just on your say-so.

The guilty secret behind every Leo Ascendant is you're a people pleaser. You want everyone to be happy with what you do. One frown from the wrong person and you'll reverse your position or start jumping through hoops to make them smile and clap again. If you want to be seen as king of the jungle instead of a circus act, you're going to have to risk people being upset with you from time to time. That's why they say heavy is the head that wears the crown.

## LEO SUN/LEO RISING

People crave your approval. They're always checking to see if you're happy with the way things are going. And should a frown cross your face then they want to know if there's something they can do to make life better. It's strange the way people defer to you. Even if they're perfectly capable of doing something on their own they'll still stop to ask for your input. It's something you've gotten used to with loved ones and friends, but it gets a little awkward when you're around experts who are clearly more knowledgeable than you.

Leo/Leo Risings are Astrology's celebrities. Everything changes when you walk into a room. People come running up to you begging for a selfie while others hang on to your every word. And then there are those who secretly wish you'd leave so life can return to normal. When you were younger you reveled in this attention, but over time you began to realize what can happen if you're not careful about where you direct your gaze. People are so easily insulted. They can tell if you're looking past them or are thinking of something else while they're talking to you and become visibly upset. When you radiate as much solar power as you do then you're on show constantly like an animal in the zoo. There's no such thing as an off day. You can't get away with anything. Other Rising Signs can bend the rules, fib, and even slip out the back when nobody's watching, but not you. You will always get caught because all eyes are on you.

Because you're so successful at the things that come naturally, it can be a shock when you say you want to try something different. It's like a sitcom actress announcing she's only going to do serious dramas from now on. Suddenly the people who were in your corner—aren't. And like a moviegoing audience they'll ignore what you're doing. This kind of ostracization can be really hard to take and many of you will return to the role you're expected to play. But for those of you willing to risk rejection and disdain—you'll find that after a while even those who were set against you will warm to you again. You're a Leo/Leo Rising. You can't help winning over their hearts.

## VIRGO SUN/LEO RISING

You are so much more than you allow yourself to be. People acknowledge it all the time when they praise you for a job well done or marvel at the way you expertly salvaged a situation. They know you are capable of great things, which is why they encourage you to raise your sights. Your response, however, is to downplay what you do. Others assume you're being modest, but actually it's a form of self-restraint. Virgo Suns with Leo Risings are a bit like werewolves struggling to keep their wild side in check. You see you're not afraid of being *seen* as egotistical; rather, you're afraid of *becoming* egotistical—dominating every conversation and sucking up all the oxygen in the room. That's why you practice rigorous humility. Resisting notice and selflessly assigning credit to someone else prevents you from transforming into an attention whore.

So when did *ego* become such a dangerous word? You'll need to go back to childhood to uncover that one. Maybe one parent had an overly inflated sense of importance that was shameless and embarrassing or the other was self-denigrating to the point of annihilation. In any case, you were left with a distorted picture where anything regarded as self-serving was immediately denounced as narcissistic.

Maybe if you were born at a time of day when the Sun was farther away from the Ascendant it would be easier to recognize the discrepancy, but the signs being right next to each other in the zodiac makes it hard to see. That's why your Virgo Sun is always on your Ascendant's case and your Leo Rising snarls back at the cracking whip.

At some point you're going to discover how counterproductive underselling yourself can be. Self-denial isn't the answer when you're better than most. You know you work harder, keep longer office hours, and are more talented. But you're the one who keeps saying you're none of these things. You're the one who keeps stooping beneath a ceiling that's too low for you to stand upright. You get nowhere fast pretending to be someone you're not and that's something your Leo Rising can't abide. If you don't want to become one of those people who never lives up to their potential, then it would be a good idea to loosen your hold and let the lion perform.

# LIBRA SUN/LEO RISING

Bold, rash, and decisive, you may have a hard time relating to the textbook description of a Libra. There's nothing about you that's noncommittal or tentative. You don't hem and haw over choices any more than you'll poll friends about what to wear that day. You have a dramatic flair, a signature look, and maybe even a personal logo. When you're a Libra Sun with Leo Rising you know your own mind and heart and nobody's going to throw you off balance.

Libra/Leo Risings are irresistibly attractive. It comes from having a Sun-ruled Ascendant (magnetic and charismatic) and a Venus-ruled Sun (exquisitely poised and tasteful). The strange thing is you don't need to be a classic beauty. If anything, you're probably not and that's exactly what people find fascinating about you. If you were to get a nose job, go on a diet, or alter your appearance in any way then you'd ruin the effect. There's a part of you that's always known this and as you've grown in confidence over the years you've come to accentuate these remarkable features of yours even more.

A lot of people talk about authenticity these days, but you're more interested in style. Style makes a statement and leaves an impression long after you've left the room. It's something people admire and want to copy. Always weighing the effect you have on others, you're constantly gauging your performance—when is it best to be understated or to exaggerate for effect. Libra/Leo Risings are often engaged in the buying and selling of high-price items. This runs the gamut from fashion to properties. You never talk about money. If a client has to inquire about the price then you'll politely volunteer that they might be better off going someplace else.

Where you are a quintessential Libra is in your endless pursuit of the perfect mate. Libras idealize relationships, and your Leo Rising is a hopeless romantic. It's an irrepressible combination because for all your exacting standards, you're quick to throw away the rule book when somebody breathtakingly beautiful walks into the room. And you will stubbornly make the same mistake time and time again by assuming too much while questioning too little. Yet for all the ensuing heartbreak and despair, it's clearly a mistake that you never get tired of making.

## SCORPIO SUN/LEO RISING

You are as compelling as you are undeniable. The gravitational pull of your Ascendant combined with the mysterious aura of your Sun Sign makes you someone everyone notices right away. There are no mixed feelings about you. People either love you or avoid you.

You may not see yourself as a domineering personality, but others do. They can sense instinctively that you're the sort of person who always wins. Whether you succeed in the moment or circle back years later to plant your flag, you will have the last word in the end. It's why so many would rather yield the field than cross swords with you.

Now this is the sort of notoriety that a Scorpio can really enjoy. You like being spooky. But where Scorpios are nocturnal by nature, your Rising Sign is pure sunlight. It wants to bask in the rays and soak up the heat. And as you can imagine there's going to be a conflict between these two different sides of your personality.

When you're on, you're on. Your smile dazzles and your eyes blaze. You move about with the glamorous stroll of a movie star on the red carpet. You know full well that you are on display and will happily give people what they want. You might even lock eyes with an admirer and shoot them a quick wink. Scorpio/Leo Risings can be delightfully cheesy.

What this covers up is a deep-rooted cynicism. Leo Risings will always play to the crowd, but Scorpios are intensely aware of how gullible people are. And instead of feeling clever, it only makes you lonely. Born under the zodiac sign of hidden agendas, you see how clumsy people are at disguising their motives. It's why they never get past the velvet rope.

You don't believe it when someone says they love you. You're constantly questioning if they truly mean it. The problem with that is the bottomless pit of angst every Scorpio carries around inside. Thankfully your Leo Rising draws people to you like a petting zoo. They're more than happy to show you more affection than you feel like returning. And in time when you see that they're not going anywhere, you might even lower your guard. Nobody's saying you have to believe their adulation, but where does it say you can't enjoy it?

## SAGITTARIUS SUN/LEO RISING

You have always been the favorite. Singled out at an early age by a parent or relative who felt no qualms about doting on you, they gushed on and on about your gifts, talents, and good looks. It was clear from the start that they took pride in you and it's this stamp of approval that you carry throughout your life. Lots of people are told all sorts of things as children that they wind up discovering aren't true when they grow up, but this recognition is so embedded in your heart that you've never doubted it for a moment. It's an unwavering faith in yourself that will always be there when you feel lost or broken.

Needless to say, it hasn't been easy. Siblings didn't appreciate being regarded as also-rans any more than friends liked being compared to you by their own parents. Being held up as a shining example of what to do right didn't always make you popular. Instead of respect and admiration, it attracted jealousy and animosity. Thankfully Sagittarius/Leo Risings are good-humored about setbacks. Your indefatigable insistence on looking at the bright side of things combined with an expertise for turning lemons into lemonade keeps you going no matter how many times you're knocked flat.

Ironically your biggest breakthroughs appear right when you've reached a dead end. That's because Sagittarius/Leo Risings come with a deus ex machina built into their horoscopes. You can be on the verge of getting evicted for unpaid rent only to hear that someone wants to buy your work or you might help out a stranger who—unbeknownst to you—is in a position to open doors for you in return. These fortuitous turns are when you are once again recognized by a person of influence who lifts you up and puts you back on the pedestal where you belong. Admittedly, there have been a few close calls over the years, but the last-minute saves never fail to deliver.

Hopefully you understand where all of this is headed. It's one thing to be true to yourself, quite another to be charged with a moral obligation to do exactly that. Fate will always put you back on the path to realizing your potential and making the most of your gifts, but you're still the one who has to take the journey.

## CAPRICORN SUN/LEO RISING

You're often asked: What are you doing working here? At first it was flattering because it made you feel special, but over time it's become kind of annoying because you like what you do for a living and don't appreciate it being frowned upon. You take great pride in the service you provide and in the extra steps you take to make sure that yours is a job well done. What you do for a living may not be the most glamorous thing, but it gives you great satisfaction. It puts food on the table, money in the bank, and a roof over your head and the heads of those you care about. Knowing that you've got everything covered and have accounted for every contingency allows you to sleep at night.

Nevertheless people will still persist in their belief that you should be doing something else. They think that you should be on TV, strutting your stuff on the runway, or cutting a single that will surely go platinum. There's something about you that strikes them as being better than the circumstances they find you in. One would think you were John F. Kennedy Jr.'s long-lost love child or the great-great-granddaughter of Princess Anastasia the way they carry on. Being a Capricorn with Leo Rising has that kind of effect. People have this expectation of greatness that doesn't allow for the fact that you're fine as is.

You trust in Time and Fortune. If something is meant to be then it will be. Now that doesn't mean you'll sit back and accept whatever the Stars dole out to you. You're a Capricorn. You put a lot of stock in hard work and a game plan that will pay off handsomely one day. But you also know—like any mountain goat—that you have to descend from one peak in order to scale a higher one, which means taking on student debt, paying your dues, or apprenticing under a harsh taskmaster if that's the only person who can train you to be the best at what it is you want to do. Capricorns seem pre-destined to take the hard way. Others may shake their heads at you choosing such an onerous course, but you know that it will all come together in the end. Your Leo Rising will make sure of that.

## AQUARIUS SUN/LEO RISING

People think you're haughty, but you're not. If anything, you believe that each voice should be heard and that all sides of the argument need to be respected, which is why you will never talk over anyone or boss them around. You see yourself as benefitting from differing perspectives yet in the end the final decision always rests with you. And that's the part that strikes people as imperious.

You're used to being the adult in the room. It's been that way since childhood. Part of this comes from the fact that Aquarians are born preter-naturally mature—you possessed a droll look even as an infant—and part of this stems from one of your parents not being around. Sunset charts of-ten indicate the early departure of a parent either physically or psycho-logically, which meant that you would have had to raise yourself. This peculiar mix of being older than your years but never having outgrown your inner child still follows you around to this day.

The combination of Aquarius and Leo makes you genuine and honest. Aquarians will always tell the truth and your Rising Sign can't hide what it feels; however, this doesn't mean that you won't try to control the flow of information. Deciding on a case-by-case basis who should know what and how much creates the impression of being totally aboveboard when actually you're not. Editing what's said and to whom can be just as misleading as an out-and-out lie, and where you get yourself into trouble is when you lose track of who knows what. The thing about life as a Leo Rising is that like the Sun, everything comes out eventually and you could wind up exposing yourself in a very public way.

The biggest mistake you make is assuming that you alone can solve a problem. It's a very Leo Rising thing to believe. That is why there will be times in your life when you will have great falls, but fortunately there are plenty of king's horses and plenty of king's men on hand to put you back together again. What you learn over time is that people are capable of handling the truth more than you think and—if given the chance—they might surprise you with how insightful and helpful they can be.

# PISCES SUN/LEO RISING

You're a natural performer whether you want to be or not. You have this gift for physically embodying others' visions. You're the character described in the script, the voice others imagine in their heads, or an ideal made flesh.

People get so excited when you're around that it would be a shame to disappoint them. And given your love for approval you'll happily oblige.

You have one of those lives filmmakers make movies about. Pisces/Leo Risings often begin without a hope in the world, soar to the top, make every conceivable mistake, and somehow wind up redeemed in the end. Whether yours is an inspiring triumph or a morality tale, you can be sure that nobody will ever hate you. Even if you were to suddenly walk away from everything you built, people would still be on your side. They can't help loving you—no matter how many hearts you break.

You're a mystery to everyone, including yourself. Left to your own devices, you'd happily spend time alone. You have no problem with silence or long directionless walks with only your thoughts for company. But that Leo Rising keeps calling you back like a stage mother who won't be disobeyed. It will come grab you by the collar and push you out in front of the curtain so that you can do that thing you do that makes people want to cheer, applaud, and spend money. And it's no coincidence that Pisces/Leo Risings are famous for going through their own money—whether it's spending sprees, unwise investments, or being swindled by those you trusted. You may feel ashamed about making such bad choices, but don't be. It's actually a mechanism built into your horoscope. It's the Stars' way of allowing you some downtime, but not too much. Once you've been away too long then circumstances will conspire to make you come back and perform again. Yours is a chart that's never meant to retire.

Pisces Sun/Leo Risings are often left wondering how much of your life is your choice and how much is devoted to fulfilling others' expectations. Actually it's a mix of the two and the sooner you can find a way to make them dovetail, the happier you will be. Adoration keeps you alive and your guilty secret is that you enjoy it.

# ARIES SUN/LEO RISING

Most people fumble around for the pause button when the alarm goes off in the morning, but you rise and shine with a brisk snap-to—eager to see what the new day will bring. There isn't a challenge you've faced or a dilemma you've wrestled with that didn't feel specifically tailored to open your heart, broaden your horizons, and raise your consciousness.

Few people live in the moment like you do. Most dwell on the past or worry about the future, but you are always connected to what's happening *now*. That's how you can greet people you see every day as if it were the first time and listen with fresh ears to their problems, travails, or complaints. Everything about you is uplifting. Your support is heartfelt, your advice insightful, and your guidance is based on what a person *can* do rather than on what they've done. But you're not high on life or blindly optimistic. You've experienced more than your share of Fate's gut punches. Yet if there's anything you've learned from crumpling to the mat it's the importance of walking away from a defeat with what's educational and leaving the rest. Falling short shows us how much further we needed to go and a weakness reveals a strength asking to be developed.

You're a peak experience person. You don't do Sturm und Drang. That's just what happens when the Sun is exalted in Aries. Yours is a springtime Sun, which means that it's young and vibrant and just starting out. There's nothing about you that's jaded or feels like you deserve more because of who you are. Respect has to be earned, admiration won, and your worth proven again and again. And it doesn't matter if you're seventy years old, you'll still enter every contest with the determination of a decathlon athlete. Admittedly you may not perform the way you used to, but that won't stop you from giving it your best shot. That can-do attitude never goes away.

You're not going to be best friends with everybody, but you will be with most. Aries/Leo Risings are one of the most personable combinations. Like the Sun rising on a new day, people can't help but turn in your direction and bask in your heat and light.

# TAURUS SUN/LEO RISING

That dazzling smile is hard to miss. It's so one of a kind that if a friend meeting you for lunch described you to the waitress she would be able to lead them right to your table. More identifiable than a laugh and captivating than a glance, your smile always gives you away. Even during those times when you're serious and focused on the task at hand, it has a way of moving up into your eyes and making them sparkle. You just can't help being the most luminescent person in the room. And given that Taurus is ruled by Venus and your Rising Sign is ruled by the Sun, there's no question that you're going to have great hair as well.

Taurus/Leo Risings are industrious and persevering. You're proud of the heavy workload you carry and often draw attention to it—like a weightlifter grunting triumphantly at the gym so everyone can see how hard they struggled. You have a commanding air and won't think twice about showing colleagues that your way is the best way to do things. And it often is because you know what you're doing. Others may accuse you of being smug or cocky, but what matters most is doing a good job. It's all about the work with you.

Respecting other people's boundaries is a lifelong lesson for Taurus/Leo Risings. It's funny that for someone who gets bent out of shape every time someone encroaches on your space, you don't think twice about encroaching on theirs. You may know what's best for loved ones and friends, but they're never going to listen unless you back off and let them make their own decisions. It may drive you crazy the way a loved one will avoid a confrontation or a friend vacillates endlessly about a situation that's a no-brainer, but you need to let them do exactly that. You need to trust that they know what's best for themselves. It's hard watching the people you care about mess up, but how else are they going to learn? If you don't let them fall flat on their faces then they're never going to learn how to pick themselves back up and try again. This belief in them may not seem like much to you, but it means the world to them.

## GEMINI SUN/LEO RISING

You're the fun one. Spontaneous, irreverent, and a tad mischievous, you're the person who gets away with everything—mocking the stuffy types, thumbing your nose at authority, and calling out the emperors parading around in their birthday suits. But you never do it in a way that's condescending or mean-spirited. It's always genial and good-humored. Clownish even. This creates the impression that you're a regular dude who's just telling it like it is and it's your candor that people find so winning. You may play dumb, but you're wickedly smart and you know an opportunity when you see it. Born at the time of day when the Sun is high in the sky but hasn't yet peaked, there's no limit to your ambition. When people ask how far you think you will go in life you tell them you'll know when you get there.

Nobody quite knows how you got to where you are today. And truth to tell, neither do you. How do you explain all the chance meetings, lucky co-incidences, and windows opening when a door just closed? You have always been fortunate when it comes to meeting the right people at the right time. Maybe it was at a party or maybe it was the buddy of the guy who broke your heart, but they're the ones who make the introductions, introduce you to a friend of a friend, or offer to show a producer your demo. There's always been a human chain between you and your good fortune and you'll never forget it.

When you're a Gemini/Leo Rising there's a tendency to treat your Rising Sign like a mask that you wear. It's a persona you can put on and take off again, but it isn't really you. Part of this comes from Gemini's famously split personality, and part of it comes from this feeling of always being on the outside looking in. You have a performer's instinct for knowing what an audience wants, but this can be a dangerous game to play—as the scores of celebrities who became eclipsed by the role they made famous can un-doubtedly attest. There's a fine line between play and "let's pretend" so make sure not to cross it because once you start referring to yourself in the third person then you know you're in deep trouble.

# CANCER SUN/LEO RISING

People are so happy to see you when you walk into the room that you often wonder whom they were waiting for. You don't remember being anyone interesting or having done something that exceeded others' expectations. Yet there they are—all smiles and adoring eyes. Just about everything you do is interpreted in the opposite way. Try claiming that what you accomplished was no big deal and you're accused of false modesty. Try saying that you'd like to be alone for a while and you'll find yourself in the middle of a group hug. People don't understand you're shy by nature and that one of the worse things anyone can do to a Cancer Sun is to shower them with praise. And it doesn't matter how many times you tell them otherwise, they'll never believe you. Sometimes it feels like you're in one of those movies where two souls switched bodies and they have to pretend to be the other until they can find a way to switch back. But in your case there is no changing back, which is why your life feels like a prolonged case of mistaken identity.

The sooner you accept that most people have no idea of who you are—and no real interest in getting to know you—the better off you'll be. You will only exhaust yourself trying to explain things. Plus, why does it matter when it's easier to play along? This is what smart people born into beautiful bodies and poetic souls with rough exteriors learned a long time ago. It doesn't matter what others think as long as you're clear on who you are. And the sooner you straighten that out, the sooner you can start turning these circumstances to your advantage.

What you need most when you're a Cancer/Leo Rising is family. But that doesn't necessarily mean your birth family. It means a close circle of friends and intimates who get you—and on a deep level. These people are your roots. The ones you can hang out with and who remind you of who you are when you feel like you've lost track. It isn't always easy being a nighttime person in a daytime body, but as long as you get your downtime and have a private space to retreat to, you'll be fine.

# VIRGO RISING

It's abundantly clear when you don't like some- **You were built to** thing. That frozen smile gives you away every **fix, not to break.** time. It's forced, tense, and as irrepressible as a knee-jerk reaction. Obviously it would be so much easier if you would just come out and say that you don't like something when you don't like it, but that's not going to happen. You're a Virgo Rising. You were built to fix, not to break; to support and not forsake, which is why you will immediately start looking for a remedy. It doesn't matter if the other person wasn't hurt by what you said or offended by your response, you won't leave it alone. And it's not like you're doing this for the approval ratings or because it pains you to see anyone disappointed. It's because you are cosmically programmed to make things better. That's why you will struggle to resuscitate situations that are best left discarded. You mean well, but instead of a quick, clean rejection that would have allowed everyone to move on, your need to salvage the situation becomes death by a thousand helpful suggestions.

You can't help helping people to help themselves. Virgo is ruled by Mercury, the messenger of the gods. The only deity able to travel from heaven to hell and back again, Mercury spent a lot of time on earth hanging out with mortal folk. In fact, Mercury was known as "the companion to man" because he was always getting people out of jams, showing them the quickest way from here to there, or retrieving lost objects. There was nothing remote about Mercury just like there's nothing removed about you. You're there for people, which is why Virgo is the zodiac sign of service.

Virgos are often accused of being purists, exacting critics who scour entire forests searching for one straight stick. This comes from Virgo's association with virginity, which is why your Rising Sign is often described as prudish—blushing at the mere mention of sex and declining to hold hands in public. It's a propaganda campaign and don't you believe it. Virgo is the only zodiac sign that symbolizes a woman, so it makes perfect sense for twenty-five-hundred years of misogyny to be heaped onto this constellation, which is why words like *manipulative*, *cold*, and *bitch* are employed to demean you. It can feel at times like there's a lot to live down or explain away, but there isn't. The biggest challenge for any Virgo Rising is to accept yourself, warts and all—even if you can already see how a little salicylic acid and maybe even a skin peel wouldn't be the worst idea.

# VIRGO SUN/VIRGO RISING

Life is full of problems and you couldn't be happier. The fact that there will always be a stumbling block, setback, or something not going off as expected means you will never be out of a job. You get so excited when someone comes to you with a mishap that you just want to give them a big hug. You're so happy they screwed up! And it's this response you've learned to repress for fear of being seen as someone who delights in others' misfortunes. It took you a long time to perfect your seriously concerned face. It hides your inside smile.

Virgos are as flippant and mischievous as any Gemini. You're both ruled by Mercury, the god of tricks. The difference, however, is confidence. Geminis never met a rule they couldn't bend whereas Virgos are terrified of getting caught. At first this made you obedient and parochial. You may have spent your young adult life meticulously coloring inside the lines, but once you gained everyone's trust and were assured that nobody was watching, you got wily. Geminis are often accused of being thieves and liars, but it's the Virgos you want to look out for. They're the planners. You work out all of your steps ahead of time so that you're in and out with no one being the wiser. There's a reason why Agatha Christie, the greatest mystery writer of all time, was born under Virgo.

Having your Sun Sign double as your Ascendant means that you're always "on." All eyes are on you as you make your entrance. Now some signs enjoy this. They like parading around in the buff—astrologically speaking. They have a "like what you see?" attitude. As a Virgo/Virgo Rising you've adopted a hide-in-plain-sight approach and have become quite adept at throwing people off the scent. You know how to dress down, misdirect, and leave behind a trail of clues that leads to the conclusion you wanted others to reach all along. And it's because you'd make such a great criminal mastermind that you're the go-to expert when it comes to figuring out why the fail-safe plan doesn't work or catching the flaw everyone overlooked. Virgo/Virgo Risings are the critical thinkers of the zodiac and you often fill positions where your contributions have never been more . . . critical.

# LIBRA SUN/VIRGO RISING

You can't help noticing when someone's in trouble. Their routine is off, they're suddenly uncommunicative, and you can tell that they're going out of their way to avoid you. Now most of us wouldn't even register that there's been a change, but you do. Your attention to detail and sixth sense for something being askew don't lie, but the challenge is in broaching the topic without spooking the person you're talking to. Libra/Virgo Risings are like people who work in animal rescue. You speak in soothing tones, never come on strong or make a grab, and will always take as long as it takes to coax someone out of their frightened corner. The end result is that you build trust, earn confidence, and always emerge with your prize in hand.

Clearly you have all the qualifications of a hostage negotiator but you're not typically drawn to high-stakes situations. Your preference is to address a matter before it becomes a problem. This isn't to nip it in the bud or stomp it out, but rather to redirect it in an organic and holistic way. As far as you're concerned there are few things in life that are so wrong that they can't be rehabilitated. This is why you're so good at talking to people who have reached the end of their rope, are ashamed by their own behavior, or feel like they can't fix what's broken. You show them that there's more rope than they think, that shame is in the eye of the beholder, and broken is the first step in a creative process. You impress others with how nonjudgmental and encouraging you can be.

This wasn't always the case. You used to be stiflingly critical and most aggressively so with yourself. But what you couldn't heal in yourself, you could heal in others and over time you learned to not get down on yourself so much. Some signs need words to help them identify who they are and what they're about; you need tools. That's why your profession isn't just a job, but an expression of who you are. It's as integrally connected to you as a paintbrush to an artist or a toolbox to a carpenter. And the better you are at what you do—which is aimed at helping people to help themselves—the better human being you become.

# SCORPIO SUN/VIRGO RISING

People often have to ask if you're being sarcastic. They can never quite tell if you meant to be funny or are absolutely serious. Your understated way of saying things can sometimes give the impression that you may be laughing at the person you're supposed to be laughing with. Always respectful and a touch self-deprecating, you can still leave this lingering impression that not everything was meant in jest.

You enjoy that people don't really know where they stand with you. You're the one person at the office who refuses to play the game. You don't have to. You can communicate more with a downward glance, a polite response, or an unseen exit than most do with all their boasts and claims and mission statements. With you it's what's *not* said that gets everyone's attention. This is how loved ones can tell you're upset, colleagues know that you're deadly serious, and even a hard-to-please boss will lean in and quietly ask if they did something wrong. You've never had to speak up or speak out because when you have something to say people stop what they're doing and listen.

Scorpio/Virgo Risings project an enormous "mind your own business" aura. It's not quite as bad as Darth Vader's signature force choke, but it's enough to get people to rethink the question or change the subject. As a result, nobody really gets close to you . . . unless invited. And once in, they discover a very different person. Not entirely different, but different enough to say that the suit doesn't match the underwear.

Scorpio isn't made any more careful because of a Virgo Rising. If anything, this combination makes you more daring because you can get away with just about anything. No one would ever suspect mild-mannered you of carrying on a torrid affair, trafficking in contraband goods, or running an escort service on the side. And even if you've never done any of these things, you've surely thought about it a lot. This is what makes Scorpio/Virgo Risings such great novelists and screenplay writers.

Finally, Scorpio/Virgo Risings are often haunted by something that occurred in early childhood having to do with the mother. Maybe it was loss, separation, or rejection. Whatever the family skeleton, you need to address it if you're ever going to be intimate with someone.

# SAGITTARIUS SUN/VIRGO RISING

You have a habit of surprising people. They're used to you spouting all kinds of kooky ideas and pie-in-the-sky aspirations; but what they're not accustomed to is how often you're right about things. You just have this innate ability to hit the mark—even when you're not trying, like a blind-folded marksman shooting a rifle over their shoulder in a Wild West show. It's hard to tell how much of this is intellectual versus what's intuitive, but you also have a knack for locating missing keys, coming up with the right word for the crossword puzzle, or speaking fluently about a subject nobody even thought you were interested in. The fact that you continue to astound those who thought they knew you best is a favorite guilty pleasure.

At first, Sagittarius and Virgo seem like an unlikely pair. How can anyone hope to yoke together a "don't fence me in" Sagittarius Sun with an "everything by the book" Virgo Ascendant? Yet what these two zodiac signs have in common is a love of learning. You never stop reading, exploring, practicing, and perfecting, and all while working a variety of jobs and juggling pressing responsibilities. You're often asked where you find the time to do it all, but in truth you think clearer and work faster when under deadline. This is why you're always on the go.

The greatest paradox may be in how much you want a family but are never around. Sagittarius/Virgo Risings tend to check out physically and/or emotionally. This can range from building people's houses but rarely being at home in your own to being on call for others while needing to hire someone to look after your kids. It seems completely self-contradictory, but this is your horoscope's way of staying true to its two masters. Sagittarius doesn't want its horizons narrowed and Virgos keep on working because they wouldn't know what to do with themselves if they stopped.

At times you can come across as hectic and harassed and then suddenly you'll surprise everybody by treating them to an unplanned vacation. You have a way of looping back into their lives right when it looks like you disappeared from view. You're the sort of friend that can pick up right where you left off after years of not having seen each other.

# CAPRICORN SUN/VIRGO RISING

You will take a forever with a project. That's why employers know better than to hand you anything last minute or that's in need of urgent attention. The way you fuss over materials, comb through the data, and fine-tune every detail would drive most people crazy. It can take you all morning to remove a comma only to decide to put it back in again that afternoon. Your process may be agonizingly tedious to others, but for you it's when time stands still and you feel most free.

A Capricorn/Virgo Rising is the perfect horoscope for rarefied occupations like a custom furniture maker, jewelry designer, or art restorer. But should you find yourself employed as a gym instructor instead, you will still invest the same kind of care and attention. You don't just post a sign-up sheet outside the weight room waiting for people to show up. You decide whom you're going to work with ahead of time based on personal interviews and physical assessments. If candidates don't meet your specific criteria then you won't take them on. Time is your most precious commodity and you're not going to waste yours on people who aren't equally committed. You are seriously hard-core about what you do and it's astonishing how clients will pay whatever price you quote. There's no disputing the top quality of your work or that you are a shrewd salesperson.

Most would think that Capricorn/Virgo Risings are impossibly stuffy, but you're actually the opposite. Outside of work you love a good time and have a bawdy sense of humor. There isn't a part of your body that you won't show off or make fun of. Famous for comments that can't be repeated in polite society, you sometimes startle people with your trashy side. People assume that it's you just letting off steam, but no, that's who you are.

You likely came from humble origins and have never lost touch with your roots. It's why you always find a way to give back as soon as you're in a position to do so. There are certain causes that you hold dear and you give to them generously. But you don't just write a check. You'll take an active role in their growth and development. You want them to be just as successful as you are.

# AQUARIUS SUN/VIRGO RISING

People rely on your assessment of a situation. Nobody can process information, weigh the pros and cons, and then map out a series of viable options faster than you. You have a solid grasp of the facts and your analysis is sound. This gives the impression that you know exactly what to do at all times, but nothing could be further from the truth. Making the case for or against something is not the same as rendering a final verdict. That's an altogether different skill set. Nothing in life is open and shut. You're too aware of the unanswered questions, the overlooked details, and the unconscious bias that lie behind the judgments most people make. You'll work hard to leave no stone unturned, but always stop short of volunteering an opinion. You prefer to lay out the evidence and let the higher-ups draw their own conclusions. You're more comfortable in positions where you advise or recommend.

You spend a lot of time trying to figure out your feelings, which is interesting because most people assume you don't have any. Aquarius and Virgo are two famously cerebral signs. One lives in its head while the other is constantly overriding its wilder impulses out of fear it's going to do something reckless. The result is you can come across as so remote and disinterested that you make Alexa sound like a gushing tween. Nevertheless you spend a lot of time either running away from or catching up to what's really going on inside. Your horoscope comes with a delayed emotional reaction, which is why people need to give you a couple of weeks to answer the question of whether you like them or not.

Many people regret their actions. You regret your *in*action. You're haunted by the times you were silent when you wanted to speak up or walked away instead of staying put. But living in the moment just isn't something you can do. Your timing doesn't work that way. Aquarius already wrestles with whether it's in or out of step with what's going on, and your Virgo Rising—with its penchant for second-guessing situations—only exacerbates it. Thankfully your horoscope is no stranger to do-overs and second chances. It doesn't matter how many wrong decisions you made when you were younger, you will always have a chance to rectify them later.

# PISCES SUN/VIRGO RISING

No one would ever guess that you're a Pisces. You're punctual, consistent, and well put together. Not exactly the qualities one associates with a zodiac sign famous for following its dreams wherever they lead and then picking up the pieces afterward as it staggers back home. A child of the sea, you are drawn to dips and rises as well as to tranquility and stillness. Your inner life is equal to—if not more than—the one you live in the open and your allegiance is to the invisible world of elective realities rather than the day-to-day grind. Yet here you are—clocking hours, making the rounds, and showing up when co-workers call in sick. So what happened?

You never stopped being a Pisces. You have a boundless imagination and an unfathomable soul; however, you were born at Sunset when the rays of the day are being gathered up and tucked away for the night. Virgo is the zodiac sign of the single mom. Many people with this Ascendant were indeed raised by an unmarried mother. She might have been abandoned, divorced, or widowed—or simply decided she'd do a better job of raising you on her own than she would with a partner. In any case, the father—like the Sun in your horoscope—was departing. Either he was always on his way out the door or just never around. Yet it's not so much the father's absence that haunts you as it is this sinking feeling that you yourself might disappear like a ship over the horizon if it weren't for the commitments, routines, and responsibilities mooring you in place.

Ironically it's your Virgo Rising that can assist in realizing your talents if you would let it. In Medieval Astrology, Mercury, Virgo's ruler, was the patron planet of artisans. It governed sculptors, painters, wood carvers, and people who made musical instruments. Mercury rules eye-to-hand dexterity, which is what's needed to produce a body of work. That along with discipline and a healthy respect for deadlines. It may feel at times like your Rising Sign acts as a babysitter, ensuring that you get your work done on time, but if you allow it to show you the ropes (literally), then you will quickly master the skills needed to make your creative vision a reality.

# ARIES SUN/VIRGO RISING

Nobody can do it right but you. That's why you're always taking over when something breaks down or coming up with the last-minute plan that saves the day. You're the person people turn to in times of need. This stems from the fact that you really do know what you're doing and everyone trusts you; however, people also know what happens when somebody else tries to handle things. You will hover around them asking if that's really the best way to proceed, point out the steps they overlooked, and pleasantly suggest a variety of methods until they give up and pass the reins over to you. It's funny how you will actively avoid going near any leadership position but won't stop questioning, challenging, and correcting until you wind up behind the wheel.

People take one look at your Virgo Rising and they see a control freak. A know-it-all. An exacting critic who won't stop kicking the tires until the entire vehicle collapses in a heap. What they don't see is the reason why. And it's not because you're a perfectionist. It's because you don't want to be under anyone's thumb.

It is the nature of your Rising Sign to be submissive. Virgos hate this about themselves, which is why they will go to great lengths to learn everybody's job along with their own. It's this institutional knowledge that gives you the final say. This is how you put bosses in their place with a glance, silence clients with a raised eyebrow, and bring a discussion to an end by never even entering it. Everyone knows not to cross a Virgo Rising even though you're still the one fetching coffee.

You're nobody's fool. Which also explains why you seek out partners who are married, workaholics, or otherwise engaged. You don't want anyone bossing you around. Getting together for a good time and then going your own separate ways afterward is your way of having your cake and eating it too. If you know that it is the nature of Aries to follow and for Virgos to serve then it makes sense to set up situations where you never lose the upper hand and where you can enjoy freedom and autonomy under everyone's noses. It's like wearing sexy underwear that nobody knows you've got on but you.

# TAURUS SUN/VIRGO RISING

You have a fresh, wholesome look. Plainspoken and uncomplicated, people often assume that you're some wide-eyed kid from the country because you're polite in an old-fashioned way and will gush on and on about others' achievements while making light of your own. You're easy to confide in and open up to because you're so agreeable and supportive. You're also eager to learn. It's why you have so many mentors in your life. Older folks just naturally want to take you under their wing. They can see that you really want to know how it is they do what they do and are truly committed to following in their footsteps. Not many people seek apprenticeships nowadays, but you do. And the masters you choose are generous with their trade secrets and formulas of success. They know that their legacy is safe with you.

Although these associations often proceed smoothly, there are times when you'll run afoul of those who think that they should be the beneficiaries of this information and not you. Mercury rules sibling rivalries and Venus-blessed Taurus is no stranger to others' jealous stares. It's fascinating watching you navigate this dicey terrain. You never get defensive or confrontational. On the contrary, you're modest and deferential. You learned a long time ago that entitled people always want what they don't have but once they get it quickly lose interest. They just need their prerogative to be recognized. Respect that and they become astonishingly cooperative. This is how giving up a prize results in you regaining it in the end.

You never stop improving. It's something Taurus/Virgo Risings hold sacred. You are the eternal students of the zodiac—always signing up for another course or workshop. The brain is a muscle too and you know that if you stop exercising it then it will grow stiff and frail. You treat your body the same way too, as anyone who's tried to interrupt your exercise routine has learned to their own chagrin. Young people seek you out as a counselor and often tell you things they won't tell their own friends. One of your greatest joys is imparting your knowledge to the next generation. It's your way of preserving a tradition and also paying it forward—benefitting younger people in the way that older people once benefitted you.

# GEMINI SUN/VIRGO RISING

You've always been good with your hands. That's why playing a musical instrument comes so easily. Where others struggle to learn the notes and practice scales, you just pick it up as you go. Your mind is quick but your physical mastery is quicker. In fact, thoughts move to your fingers so reflexively that it's like they have a mind of their own. You have this same talent with drawing, gaming, computing, and prestidigitation. More artisan than artist, you pride yourself on invention rather than inspiration.

There's nothing mysterious about what you do. It's all about refining your talent and perfecting your skill.

One of the great pluses to being a Gemini/Virgo Rising is that you will stick with something. Geminis aren't known for their long attention spans. You quickly lose interest in what you're doing and will happily pursue the next bright shiny object that crosses your path—more out of relief than curiosity. Geminis are always looking for ways to get out of something. It's your Virgo Ascendant, however, that combs the surface of a familiar routine searching for a new facet. Virgos delight in process. Maybe it's a variation on a theme, imposing limitations by removing certain elements, or doing something in reverse. Anything that mixes it up. Experimentation and playfulness get you to recognize fresh ways to apply what it is you do. But these paths to discovery can't be too open-ended. Virgo is an earth sign after all, which means you are results driven. You have to have something to show for yourself at the end of the day.

Geminis—like the other air signs, Libra and Aquarius—tend to be mind over matter in their approach to life. Adopt a positive attitude, insist that there's an explanation for everything you encounter, and nothing can trip you up. Yet it's your Virgo Ascendant that insists that your body be regarded as an equal partner. Acknowledging when you're exhausted, realigning your posture, remembering to breathe, and trusting in your instinctual feel for a situation does more to dissolve mental blocks than powering through them. Your body is the being that cradles your mind and to neglect it is to silence something that knows more about life and living than you could ever conceive of intellectually. Treat it right and it will return the favor.

# CANCER SUN/VIRGO RISING

Most people say there aren't enough hours in the day. As far as you're concerned, there aren't enough hours in the night. You're always talking about when you can go back to bed. Your tendency to nap during a crisis or yawn in the middle of a heated conversation has led some friends and co-workers to wonder if you might not be narcoleptic. You aren't. You just have this preternatural ability to log off when things get repetitive, like a mobile phone switching to low-power mode to conserve its battery life. You've even been caught snoring during yoga class. But this doesn't happen because you're lazy. On the contrary, you're enormously productive. It's just that sleep is where you do your best thinking.

Cancer is ruled by the Moon—the storehouse of our feelings and memories. The Moon lights the night just as the Sun lights the day. The Moon remembers who you are. That's why it's the planet of habits and routines—the things we repeat every day without a second thought—as well as the planet of traditions and genetic predispositions—things that are passed down invisibly from one generation to the next. The Moon orients us when we're lost, just like our eyes adjusting to the dark. This is why you gather, archive, and collect. You'd never toss out a keepsake even if it was given to you by an ex. Objects are more than just sentimental. They're artifacts linking you to the past like footprints that can never be covered up or washed away. Artifacts that are meant to be preserved for the future.

The Moon, like Mercury, the ruler of your Ascendant, is a planet of messages. Mercury rules over speedy thoughts and abbreviated words like tweets and texts while the Moon rules over dreams with all of their confused logic and garbled imagery. You have a unique gift to make sense of all this. Cancer/Virgo Risings often show up as psychologists, researchers, and pediatricians. You have a way with children and can appeal to the child within the most taciturn adult. You are excellent at interpreting, deciphering, and decoding. But perhaps your greatest talent is writing. Your extraordinary observations and attention to detail are so personalized that readers feel as if you are speaking to them in their own words and voice.

# LEO SUN/VIRGO RISING

How is it that you can be the CEO of a successful company and still feel treated like a temp? And what's worse is that you'll respond like one— organizing people's lunch orders, making sure that everyone's happy with what they got, and cleaning up after them when they're through. But this is more than just a self-esteem issue. It goes to the fact that you have a real problem with being seen for who you are. Deep down you know you're special, but it feels like your light is hidden under a bushel. That's because Virgo is the zodiac sign of work and service. You can't help but jump to it when someone asks you to fetch something. You're kind of like Cinderella before she meets her fairy godmother.

The biggest lesson for a Leo/Virgo Rising to learn is status. If you're a Leo then you're probably really good at something most people can't do. You may specialize in a certain line of work or you're the undisputed expert in your field. It's something that should bring in the big bucks but you constantly undersell yourself. And that's a problem that's endemic to all Virgo Ascendants. You think that offering cheap rates and working long hours will show how much you care but all it does is invite people to take advantage of you.

Stop being so accommodating. Virgo Risings tend to have a real problem looking someone in the eye. They look down or off to the side when they're spoken to. This communicates subservience. What you need to do is to tap into that inner Leo haughtiness that insists that people come to you and not vice versa. Recognize that you are one of a kind, take command of your situation, and you'll soon see how much others need you more than you need them. Sure, you may have to fire some customers who still treat you like the hired help, but you're sure to get new ones who will pay top dollar because no one delivers like you do. It's a hard thing to learn, but if Cinderella is ever going to become queen of the realm one day then she needs to steer clear of the cinders—even if that means sitting on her hands while the palace maids clean out the fireplace.

# LIBRA RISING

You have a kind face. There's something about it that's benevolent and understanding. Saintly almost. That's why feuding parties will suddenly turn to you in the heat of an argument and start to explain their grievances to you—even if you've never met before. They instinctively know that you will somehow put things right. And it's not because you have the answers or are particularly good at solving others' problems. It's more like a calming effect. Libra is the zodiac sign of weighing things in the balance, and as you stand there—listening—tempers begin to lower, voices become less strained, and reason quietly returns to the conversation—and all with you having hardly said a word.

People don't like to see you upset. And it's not an angry outburst they fear or the welling up of tears that worries them. It's the fleeting look of disappointment. It doesn't last for very long, maybe a millisecond at most, but that's all that's needed to signal to them that they have fallen in your estimation. This is more crushing than any guilt trip could ever hope to be. Anyone who's ever seen that expression never wants to experience it again.

Libra Risings make the world a beautiful place. Venus rules your Ascendant so you know what looks good on someone, how to transform the dull into the desirable, and you can instantly calculate a wine pairing for any given meal. You were predestined to be cultured and refined—even if you

**Libra Risings make the world a beautiful place.** didn't want to be at first. Because Venus rules the law of attraction and your Rising Sign is your horoscopic face, you would have drawn people into your life who saw your potential. Like an army of Henry Higginses they descended upon you—tutoring, training, and sculpting you into becoming a better version of yourself. Maybe you secretly wanted to be that person they saw and maybe not. It doesn't really much matter because you would have followed anyway regardless of your Sun Sign. Their vision of you was more beautiful than anything you could have come up with on your own. And this is the drawback to being a Libra Rising. You can't seem to get anywhere own your own. You need a partner beside you. And that partner can either lift you up or bring you down. This is why you can never be too choosy about whom you get into bed with—either romantically or professionally. Once you commit— and it takes you a long time to commit—you will stand by your relationship and do whatever it takes to make it work.

## LIBRA SUN/LIBRA RISING

You tend to attract domineering people. It's your least favorite personality type, yet there they are on your front doorstep—pestering you for an answer, begging for a commitment, or doing whatever they can to wrangle a "yes" out of you. It's exhausting and tedious but you also never really tell them to stop. This leads them to think that they still stand a chance no matter how many times you thought you had implied otherwise. It would be so much easier if you would just cut ties, but you won't. That would be rude. Besides, you can't help wondering if they see something in you that you don't or are responding to feelings that you are as yet unaware of. If you were a fire sign rising then you'd bask in all the attention, but you're an air sign, which means you're looking for a connection but aren't too sure about what's going on with you emotionally.

In Astrology, relationships are ruled by the element of air, while love is ruled by water. The reason they say love is unconditional is that you don't have to have someone in your life to feel it. You can harbor a secret crush, fantasize about a soul mate, or reminisce about someone you miss and experience love without that person being present. A relationship doesn't work like that. It needs another person. You can't be together if you're alone. That's why air signs crowd their days with contacts and acquaintances—constantly meeting, greeting, and networking. And when you're a Libra/Libra Rising you're always on the lookout for your ideal partner. But the nature of air is cerebral, while the nature of water is emotional—which is why you often end up with people who look good on paper, but whom you're not really sold on. You're kind of secretly hoping that they might have a clearer idea of why you're supposed to be together.

You're too polite for your own good, which is why you need to practice saying no. It clears the field and narrows down the choices, giving you the distance and objectivity you crave. And the wonderful thing about being born under the zodiac sign of good manners is that there are thousands of ways to let someone down softly if you're clever enough to think of them.

## SCORPIO SUN/LIBRA RISING

You accepted long ago that you will never have what you truly want. There's something built into your life that seems predestined to thwart you at every turn. What else would explain falling in love with people who don't love you back? Making sacrifices that never pay off or pursuing dreams that remain stubbornly out of reach? It isn't easy reworking your approach again and again only to come up short. Most people would feel embittered and broken—and truth to tell you've had your less-than-stellar moments—but you've always been a good sport. Never one to sulk, you're the first to congratulate others on their good fortune even if it comes at the expense of your own.

People don't become better people by getting what they want. They may be successful, but that doesn't mean they treasure what they have. In many ways your disappointments have deepened you as a person. Not only do you persevere when others give up, but you've learned to make the most of what you have *now*. This has made you enormously creative. You didn't voluntarily choose to take the harder course in life, but outfitted with the resilience of your Scorpio Sun and the clear-sightedness of your Libra Rising you will go further than you would had things worked out as expected.

So what explains the disconnect between desire and result? It's the fact that Libra and Scorpio sit next to each other in the zodiac. This creates a blind spot between signs. Imagine sitting beside someone on a tightly packed subway train. You can feel the person next to you, but you can't really see their face unless you were to turn your head abruptly in their direction, which may result in them looking back at you with a puzzled expression. Signs next to each other feel each other but they don't see each other—and that leaves room for miscues and bad judgment. Libra's nature is to let the other person go first, which essentially forfeits Scorpio's advantage, while Scorpio's insistence on concealing any sign of vulnerability prompts Libra to politely change the subject right when the need to express your feelings matters most. Speak up when you don't want to and push forward when you're dying to retreat and you'll get these contradictory sides of yourself to work in tandem.

# SAGITTARIUS SUN/LIBRA RISING

Things come easy for you. They have since you were a kid. Precious opportunities fall into your lap, wayward circumstances always click into place, and no matter the wrinkle everything works out in the end. It's like driving down a long city avenue without hitting a red light once. And this doesn't happen because you're especially respectful or devout. If anything, you're irreverent and reckless. But the combination of influences—Venus rules Libra and Jupiter rules Sagittarius—means that Fortune smiles on you like a doting parent. Other people worry about their luck running out, but you know it will always be there. You can feel it like a gentle hand squeezing yours even in the darkest times.

It's the Libra Rising that keeps you from turning into a spoiled brat. It summons special friends into your life who balance you. They're the ones who gently reprimand you when you're out of line, act as your voice of conscience when you're contemplating something unwise, and who remember the things you forgot on your climb up the ladder of success. These friends mean the world to you. They're responsible for you making the most of your talents instead of wasting them.

Sagittarian Suns are in no hurry to settle down. Wild and fun, you know that you could hook up with just about anyone you like—and you do! But your commitment-phobia doesn't come from being a romantic idealist or defending your freedom like it was a moral prerogative; it comes from your insistence on finding the right person. You know there's someone out there meant for you but the problem with many Sagittarians is that there's a lot of searching without much finding. But don't worry. You don't have to find your partner; your partner will find you.

Chances are it's the person not taken in by your charms; the one who rolls their eyes at your jokes, yawns during your stories, and refuses to take you seriously. One would think it's a match made in hell, but there's no denying that it's love at first sight—although it will take a while for both of you to accept it. But don't worry. You will. When you're a Sagittarius/Libra Rising you're not looking for a horse whisperer; you want someone who can hop aboard and ride things out.

# CAPRICORN SUN/LIBRA RISING

You're surprisingly approachable. It doesn't seem that way from across the room where you appear poised and distant, but up close you're gracious, solicitous, and always complimentary. You have a way of making others feel special and at ease. It's quite an accomplishment given that you're better dressed than most, well-read, and clearly more cultured. You wear your good manners like a custom-tailored suit expertly fitted to show you off from every angle. Not many can be so elegant without coming across as snobbish or pretentious. Instead you inspire people to stand a little taller, to ask after others before talking about themselves, and to actually go and watch that Fellini film you were praising so lavishly. Yet despite being disarmingly conversational, most people haven't the faintest idea of who you really are.

Are you like this at home? Do you breeze around the house in a chiffon robe? Are you truly the genteel person that you appear to be or do you kick your pets when nobody's looking? It's hard for others to imagine what you're like "unplugged," but the simple truth is you're the same person in public as you are in private. This is great for anyone who's been invited over for tea, quite different for loved ones living in your dollhouse.

Capricorn/Libras don't like fighting. Voices are never raised, differences are always reconcilable, and you believe that everything should be talked out. It sounds good in theory, but your Libra Rising also insists on the other person going first—even if you have to sit there waiting in silence—and on not responding right away. You want time to think things through. But even though you say that your response will be forthcoming, it can often take days or even weeks. Libras are instinctually nonconfrontational and Capricorns are famous for procrastinating. This results in conversations that should have taken place on the spot instead taking place years later in therapy.

Nothing good comes from being polite to a fault. It puts you under unnecessary stress which you internalize, being a midnight Sun. This can result in health problems and people leaving you because they didn't think you cared. Nobody's saying you have to lose your shit (you never would), but there's nothing wrong with stepping down off the pedestal from time to time and being a human being.

# AQUARIUS SUN/LIBRA RISING

You are a political animal, always collecting names, nurturing contacts, and expanding your network of friends. Those who enter your social orbit always emerge with more than what they came in with. People don't feel used or exploited by you. If anything, they're usually flattered by your willingness to open doors and make introductions. You have a sixth sense for matching the talents of one person with the capabilities of another. You have produced many successful collaborations—and each one's grateful for what you did to bring them together. It all looks casual and in-the-moment but the truth is yours is a painstakingly constructed constellation of alliances with you at the center. You know everybody. The ones people need to know and the ones they've yet to find out about.

Yet for all of your social niceties, you're still a nonconformist at heart. In fact the careful cultivation of personalities who inhabit your universe isn't meant to advance your interests, but to change the world around you. Deliberately mixing and matching people from all walks of life shakes up the status quo, expands everyone's horizons, and introduces all kinds of possibilities. Aquarius/Libra Risings may be regulars on the party circuit, but you're also just as likely to show up in think tanks, art collectives, or opening up a Montessori school in the neighborhood. Nothing's more intoxicating than the fresh pursuit of a new idea.

Yet for all this harnessing of people power, it's ironic how little you know about what makes them tick. And this isn't because you live in your head or are three steps ahead of the game. Aquarius/Libra Risings have a problem with intimacy. Always focused on the welfare of others, you find it hard to be there for the people in your life without it feeling like an obligation. Loved ones can't help but wonder when it will be their turn to receive the attention you shower on everyone else and if being in close proximity to you is something that works against them.

When you're an Aquarius/Libra Rising, you need to practice being close. And you can begin by making time in your schedule for that special someone. It will seem awkward at first—maybe even inconvenient—but given time it will become routine and your heart will open without you worrying about it so much.

# PISCES SUN/LIBRA RISING

You are too beautiful for this world. That's why people treat you like a precious metal or the last surviving member of an endangered species. There's this feeling that once you're gone then that's it. Everything that was profound and soulful vanishes with you. Some see you as sleepy-eyed and listless—in desperate need of being roused from your stupor—while others see you as poetic and wise. They're the ones who watch over you and make sure that anyone who means you harm never gets the chance. It's remarkable how you can attract hostility and command such loyalty at the same time. It's as much a mystery to others as it is to you.

Pisces people are enigmatic. It's clear that you care quite deeply and yet you won't say anything—trusting instead in the flow of the emotional current. If things are meant to work out then they will. And if not? Then it was probably for the best. This passive acceptance is hard for others to understand. It flies in the face of a society that believes in fighting for what you want. Yet you have learned that fighting only causes pain and that in the end what's best for you may not be what's best for the other person. This is something that's reinforced by your Libra Rising. Yours is the most permissive of Sun Sign/Rising Sign combinations, but permissive doesn't mean you aren't judgmental.

For someone who's as serene as a Buddhist statue, you do a lot of thinking about people and their troubles. Sometimes you're bewildered by the fixes they get themselves into and sometimes you envy them their single-minded focus that shuts out any other point of view. You are not indifferent to others' plights any more than you will let yourself be drawn into them. Instead you treat them like parables; learning opportunities, if you will. Nevertheless you will act to defend someone who cannot defend themselves. Libra is a sign of justice after all.

Perhaps the greatest blessing of being a Pisces/Libra Rising is to have one foot in the moment and one foot outside of it at the same time. This allows you to shift your weight from one to the other depending on where you need to be. This gives you the acuity of an intellectual along with the sensitivity of an artist.

## ARIES SUN/LIBRA RISING

You come across as a pretty together person. Confident and forthright, there's never a question about where people stand with you. They'll find that out in the first five minutes. You believe in speaking your mind and expressing what you feel. What's the point of holding back? As far as you're concerned it's a disservice to the other party not to be totally honest. Yet you do this all amiably. You're never dismissive or mean-spirited. The fact that you can dress down someone with the same friendly smile that you use to build them up speaks to your being evenhanded in all dealings. If you and someone click—great! You know you found someone who's simpatico. And if not? Then you don't see why you can't part company in the same positive spirit that brought you together in the first place. This is what makes you everyone's favorite person to break up with. You don't hold grudges against exes and you're fair in divorce settlements. Yes, your heart has been broken more times than you can recall but that won't stop you from searching for that special person you know is out there.

Nobody is as chivalrous as you. When people talk about their knights in shining armor they're definitely describing an Aries/Libra Rising. You don't think twice about holding the door open, giving up your seat, or taking off your coat to wrap around someone's shivering shoulders. Not only are you the first to rescue a damsel (or dude) in distress, but you can also recite poetry and strum a guitar while nursing them back to health. A mix of charm and bravado, you are a true troubadour. And like the troubadours of old, you have a penchant for falling in love with people who are already married or in a relationship with somebody else. It's a detail often omitted when sharing your romantic resume.

Knights never stayed in one place for very long. They may have had a seat at the Round Table but their butts were rarely in it. It's something to think about before signing on for your next adventure. Ask yourself how many quests have actually resulted in your finding something? It's cool if you're just into being on the road, not so cool if you've got someone at home waiting.

# TAURUS SUN/LIBRA RISING

It's hard feeling beholden to someone else. Maybe your parents are well-to-do, your spouse is financially successful, or your business is kept afloat through the good graces of an angel investor. These are the people funding your life, not you. And it doesn't matter how hard you work or how accomplished you are, you never seem to generate the kind of income that allows you to become self-sufficient. It always falls short of the mark.

Now most people would ask: What's wrong with somebody else footing the bill or supporting you in the lifestyle to which you've become accustomed? Taurus is an earth sign and earth signs don't like owing anyone anything. It's why you always pay your way, settle accounts on time, and never allow yourself to go into debt. Some might say it's a control thing, but it's really a self-worth thing. Money to a Taurus is like sex to a Scorpio or shopping to a Gemini. You're really good at it. So when you're not able to earn your keep you're going to feel like something's wrong with you. You're supposed to acquire commodities, not be one.

The issue here is Venus. Taurus and Libra are both Venus-ruled signs, but the way your Taurus Sun expresses Venus energy is very different than your Libra Ascendant. Taurus wants to amass a huge fortune while Libra wants to amass people who amass huge fortunes. In effect your Rising Sign is doing its job by pairing you with those who have already done the hard work, but what your Libra Ascendant doesn't get is that you like working.

Venus is the planet of partnering. Its focus is on bringing two people together so you get twice as much done for half the effort while benefitting everyone involved. It's hard for a Taurus to accept because you see yourself as a provider. Anything else feels like taking. But switch the mind-set from trying to keep up to what you bring to the table. Money isn't the only currency. There are other things like good ideas, emotional support, and sound advice. Meanwhile make the money you make and honor it for what it is—no matter how small. Do this and you will see things grow over time because a Libra Ascendant always ensures that things balance out in the end.

# GEMINI SUN/LIBRA RISING

You can't help wondering if you can do better. Ever since you were a child you wanted to hang out with the kids who were going places instead of the ones who watched from the sidelines. And this wasn't because you were an elitist—although you're often accused of that. Geminis are only as good as the company they keep. If you hang out with also-rans you become an also-ran, whereas if you hang out with people who challenge you intellectually and refuse to lower their sights then you will do the same. You may even outgrow them—which might explain the vague uneasiness that creeps into friends' voices when they see you fraternizing with someone new. Are they about to be replaced with the 2.0 version?

You were born with a hungry mind. Not only do you devour tweets, texts, and reels, you have an insatiable appetite for mental stimulation. That's why you'll never be satisfied with just one job, one relationship, or even one place to live. You are constantly on the go. If properly channeled this can produce an exciting career in media, sales, or even law. If not? Then this can descend into infighting, feuds, and litigious lawsuits. Gemini is a competitive sign by nature and that isn't softened one bit by the Libra Rising. If anything, it becomes subtler.

So does this make you a snake in the grass? It would if you didn't wind up becoming best friends with the people you envy. There's a strange symbiotic relationship that develops between you and someone who has something you want. There's no question that you're rivals, but this person will still come talk to you about their spouse you're in love with or ask you for guidance with the job that should be yours. And you'll help out every time. Some might say that this is dysfunctional, but there's actually something inexplicably intimate about being taken into this person's confidence, and that confidence is something you'll never break.

Meanwhile, be careful about losing the alternatives for the options. Your Libra Rising is bad enough when it comes to making a decision—add your Gemini Sun to the mix and you can't help responding to an answer with another question. This can lead to days (if not decades) of chasing your own tail.

## CANCER SUN/LIBRA RISING

You are an excellent reader of people. You can decipher their moods, intuit their thoughts, and even predict what they're going to do next. Some swear that you possess telepathic powers, but the truth is you're a keen observer. You speak fluent body language. You pick up on the nuances others miss and know that if you wait long enough then the person you're speaking to will eventually divulge all. It may not be in today's conversation or next week's, but it will come out. And the best part is you didn't do a thing to force the issue. People tell you what they want to tell you when the time is right.

It isn't easy being perceived as passive in an overly aggressive world. Cancers believe that discretion is the better part of valor and Libras are famous for leaving the decision-making up to others. This can create the impression that you're a pushover. Nothing could be further from the truth because both your Ascendant and Sun Sign are cardinal in nature. You don't take orders; you give them. However, not all cardinal signs butt heads like an Aries or climb over people like a Capricorn. The way you go about achieving your goals involves playing along, letting people believe what they want to believe, and even allowing superiors to take credit for the things you did. This never ceases to enrage loved ones and friends who feel like you capitulate all too easily, but what they fail to recognize is how you always come out ahead. Cancer/Libra Risings believe that you have to give to get and the best gift you can give is the feeling that you can be trusted. Why storm an enemy castle when a little TLC will get them to drain the moat and lower the drawbridge instead?

Noontime Cancer Suns always feel like they're out of their element. You worry that you've climbed too high or are in danger of being burned. You yearn to return to your private life every chance you get, yet you are often a success in spite of yourself because people are drawn to your work. There's just something about what you do and the way you do it that resonates on a deep level. Cancer/Libra Risings are the people whisperers of the zodiac.

# LEO SUN/LIBRA RISING

You're a people pleaser. You know what makes them happy. You can tell how much face time they need, what to compliment them on, and you never arrive at a dinner party or date empty-handed. There's always some kind of gift that you specifically selected for the occasion. It's funny how *people pleaser* is considered to be a derogatory term nowadays, but not in your case. And that's because you're not trying to make everyone like you. They already do. When you're a Leo/Libra Rising, the last thing you ever have to worry about is being popular. Crowned with a solar halo and the glamour of Venus, you will *always* be in demand.

Joy is disarming. And the fact that you are always upbeat, delighted by others' accomplishments, and genuinely wish them well makes it hard for haters to bring you down. If anything, the more holes they try to poke in your dreams and aspirations, the more petty and jealous they appear. Beauty has a funny way of bringing out the ugly in others and exposing it for what it is.

The thing to keep in mind when you're a Leo Sun/Libra Rising, though, is maintaining the balance between give and take. People automatically orbit you when you're a Leo, you don't orbit them. And this isn't an ego thing. It's a magnetism thing. When you have a charismatic personality like you do then you attract people naturally. However, some may grow resentful about how they always have to go to you about something rather than the other way around. That may sound trivial, but it's actually a big deal because resentment can build over time without you knowing it. Thankfully your Libra Rising is quick to rectify a faux pas once it's been brought to your attention and it will immediately reciprocate a favor, extend an invite, or make a goodwill gesture.

It doesn't take much to win someone back—loved ones and friends hate to be upset with you. You could sweet-talk the Cheshire Cat down out of its tree, which is why you have to be careful not to press your luck. Taken separately Leo and Libra are faithful and true, but together? There's a tendency to want to have your cake and eat it too—and this often extends to the entire dessert cart.

# VIRGO SUN/LIBRA RISING

Why does every relationship feel like an arranged marriage? Are these holdover memories from a past life or is your resistance to giving yourself over to someone that deeply ingrained? Virgo is a bundle of contradictions. Famously self-sufficient, you will never rely on anyone for anything. Even if someone picks up the tab you will insist on splitting it. And if it's more than you can afford, then you will make arrangements to pay them back. You refuse to owe anyone anything. Yet you were also born under the zodiac sign of service, which means that you can't say no to someone in need. And this isn't because you're self-sacrificing, have a big heart, or suffer from low self-esteem. You just naturally want to help. It's all you can do to *not* help the server clear the plates when dining out.

Yet for all of your prickliness, people still pursue you. It could be a romantic interest you keep turning down, an uppity supervisor who's convinced you're right for the job, or a well-heeled client who sweetens the deal every time you speak. And this is the difficulty with having Libra

Rising. Nobody believes you when you reject them. They think that you're just playing hard to get. And after a while they wear you down. It's not something you're proud of—caving into love, security, or a handsome fee—but you're a Libra Rising. You're cosmically consigned to be in a relationship. You can't get to where you want to go in life without one.

That's why it's best to work with your Ascendant rather than against it. Instead of writing out a list of terms that the other person has to agree to or endlessly itemizing what's mine versus yours so there's a tally, you might try embracing the idea that your relationship should be balanced. You're a couple. If you're overly reliant on your partner or if your partner is too demanding then you will lose that balance. If you're always running away and your partner is constantly giving chase then you will never connect. Virgos expend a lot of energy worrying about what's wrong. It comes from having a critical mind. Try spending more time recognizing what's right. You may discover a more balanced perspective and that you have more going for you than against.

# SCORPIO RISING

♏

You're the first to make eye contact. And once met, you will hold it for longer than what's comfortable. This is your way of asserting yourself without saying a word. It conveys to the other person that you mean business. You might be warning them not to mess with you, that now's the time to come clean, or you're looking to hook up. Your steady gaze is intense and penetrating and one is never quite sure if they're interpreting it correctly.

You're the first to make eye contact.

Scorpio Risings make people uncomfortable. You've been doing it since grade school when the other kids would ask you what you were staring at. Back then you probably didn't know how powerful your gaze could be. You may have been looking at the other kids longingly—wanting to join in all the playground fun—little realizing that you were coming across as vaguely menacing. This comes from having a Rising Sign that's ruled by Pluto, named after the Roman god of the underworld. Pluto had a tendency to make his celestial siblings uneasy, which is why he didn't come aboveground much. It's kind of like bringing your pit bull to the dog park. It doesn't matter how many times you say your dog is friendly, everyone is going to keep a safe distance. When you're a Scorpio Rising it's very important that you understand the way that you come across to people—especially when nine out of ten will assume that you're up to no good. You need to be ready to deal with that.

Now some Scorpio Risings relish having a dangerous reputation. You're the ones who wear a baleful expression, sport piercings in undisclosed places, and like to show off your pet tarantula at dinner parties. But for those of you born under more happy-go-lucky zodiac signs, this Ascendant can be a stumbling block. It makes people question if you're really as harmless as you say. Presumed guilty before being found innocent is nothing new for you, which is why you never want to be forced to defend yourself. The best thing is to look that dubious supervisor or suspicious love interest straight in the eye and ask them *why* they think that? This does one of two things. It either gets them to back off or to start talking about what they wanted to talk about all along. There's something about a Scorpio Rising that prompts people to share their unspoken desires, family skeletons, or criminal past—whether you wanted to hear about it or not. They just know that somehow you know what it's like and that their secret is safe with you.

## SCORPIO SUN/SCORPIO RISING

You never say what your sign is. And it doesn't matter how much people poke and prod, you still won't give up the goods until finally—and only after hours of guessing—you'll answer: "Gemini." It's a lie, but you don't care because you know from experience that the only thing worse than being a Scorpio is to be a double Scorpio. Say that out loud and you'll have every sexually adventurous soul in the room hitting on you.

For some reason people think that you're always thinking about sex. You are. But not in the sense of always looking for action. When you're a Scorpio/Scorpio Rising you're driven more by obsession than passion. You have a surly expression, a badass swagger, and an animal magnetism that people go home and fantasize about. That's why they're always scheming to be alone in the same room as you. But like Heathcliff fixated on his Cathy, your focus is on the person who got away. It's the heartbreak you never recover from, no matter how much you pretend otherwise.

You're often accused of using people to get what you want. Many say that you're amoral, premeditated, or manipulative. It's true that you have a single-minded approach to life. Nobody spends as much time calculating all the different ways to accomplish a goal or exact revenge as you do, but you never force someone to do anything against their will. You don't threaten or humiliate, however you will coax and coerce. Pluto ruling both your Sun and Ascendant makes you an expert at sniffing out others' ulterior motives. You know all about the things they want but won't admit. Does it make you evil to use their desires as a means to your ends? Scorpio/Scorpio Risings are extremely just. Anyone who goes into business with you will get what they deserve. Sometimes it's good and sometimes it's not and this is where Scorpio/Scorpio Risings aren't always kind. You know that people can be driven by dark furies in the moment that they may regret later. You could warn them ahead of time, but don't. If you learned to make peace with your inner demons then they can learn to make peace with theirs.

# SAGITTARIUS SUN/SCORPIO RISING

You keep coming back—no matter how many times you're cut down. And it's always bigger and stronger than before. Some might say that you're a glutton for punishment while others marvel at your indomitable spirit, but what's certain is that there's something about the difficulties you face that activates a hidden enzyme found only in your Sun Sign/Rising Sign combination. This mysterious quality attracts life challenges that threaten to grind you underfoot but are also necessary for unlocking the spiritual power locked inside you. You realized a long time ago that you can't have the transformation without the ordeal, which is why you run toward a crisis instead of away from it.

You were not meant for lesser things. Upbringings are often humble for Sagittarius/Scorpio Risings. There's something about the time of day you were born that seems predisposed to generating horoscopes meant to travel far from where they began. If not physically, then creatively or spiritually. The person you came into the world as bears little resemblance to who you'll become. You may wind up with a different name, living in a foreign land, or going through so many booms and busts that it's hard to remember which success defined you most. When you're a Sagittarius/Scorpio Rising you're always evolving into something different but innately familiar. And it doesn't matter if you haven't the faintest clue as to how things will turn out because you know you'll end up where you were meant to be all along.

You have a voracious appetite. It's why you grab more than you can possibly use. You order more food than you need, buy more clothes than you'll wear, and bed more lovers than you can name. Scorpio Risings don't usually do things in excess, but they can do things to the extreme. Pair this with a Sagittarius Sun that believes it's better to have too much than too little and is it any wonder why you struggle with your weight, finances, and neighbors not talking to you because you seduced their spouses? Thankfully you're the sort of person that people would rather have in their life than not. Maybe it's your exuberance or passion. Then again, maybe it's the way you live your life with a gusto that they wish they had.

# CAPRICORN SUN/SCORPIO RISING

People trust Tauruses with their money, Cancers with their children, and Virgos to organize their lives, but they leave the serious business to you. You're the one in charge of taking care of the sensitive stuff. Not only do you know where the bodies are buried, you remember how they got there. Famously inscrutable and unflinching, you don't think twice about having the meetings your client can't or handling the delicate negotiations that queasy types shy away from. You're the closer. You clean up the messes, tie up loose ends, and settle any unfinished business. That's why you're listed in so many living wills as the designated plug puller. You're the person people count on when things are down to the wire.

Your boss is everything to you. You would do anything for this person. In fact, people often comment on how you two are joined at the hip. You're there at every business meeting, working side by side until all hours of the night, and seated next to the family at weddings and funerals. This is often mistaken for subservience, but it's not. Your boss doesn't make a move or finalize a decision without consulting you first. Yours is an intensely creative collaboration. Anyone who wants to be in a relationship with you needs to accept that your boss comes first.

But not all Capricorn/Scorpio Risings are fixers or bodyguards. There's a soft side too that only comes out in private. You may have a love of knitting, a talent for restoring antiques, or you volunteer your time mentoring children with learning differences. It's something that people never find out about and you like to keep it that way. You need a special place where you can unwind and be a kinder, gentler version of yourself. Hobbies and extracurricular activities are the perfect outlet considering the pressure you're under and tough calls you're asked to make.

You dream of the day when you can leave your harried life behind, but that won't happen. You're just not built for it. Your horoscope is drawn to stressful situations like a performer seeks the spotlight or a mystic retreats into silence. This is where you come to life. You do best in relationships where your mate is just as busy as you. That makes your downtime together all the more precious.

# AQUARIUS SUN/SCORPIO RISING

It's never a good idea to lie to an Aquarius/Scorpio Rising. You were gifted with a BS meter so finely tuned that it's been dinging nonstop since your mom first told you about Santa Claus. Better than a UV light and more telling than a forensic analysis, you are constantly picking up on people's body language, word choice, and the traces that they leave behind. A Scorpio Rising never misses a trick. Add your Aquarius Sun to the mix and the result is someone who never stops factoring in every possibility, alternative, and what-if. Any cybersecurity firm worth its threat-detection infrastructure would be happy to have you on board.

Truth is a big deal to an Aquarius/Scorpio Rising. If two people have nothing to hide then there should be no problem with saying what's on your mind, texting every thirty minutes to check in, or willingly subjecting yourself to a thorough cross-examination of the days' events. But not all loved ones feel comfortable living with a human surveillance camera and that's where you need to lighten up. Someone isn't withholding information because they guard their privacy any more than they're sneaking out on you by spending time with friends. Aquarius/Scorpio Risings try to play the disinterested statistician, but the truth is you have deeply embedded trust issues.

You're never going to just let it all hang out. It's one of the most popular misunderstandings about Aquarius. People think you're laid back and hippy-dippy but you're actually wound pretty tight. You have a lot of nervous energy, live in your head (hence the bouts of insomnia), and walk a fine line between Cartesian mechanics and chaos theory. There are times when you embrace a button-down existence and then suddenly go in the opposite direction where you want nothing to do with your former self. These pendulum swings from controlled to crazed to controlled again take place once every seven years without warning.

You ask a lot from the people in your life. You keep saying they're free to come and go as they please but clearly they're not. The fact that you're possessive one moment and then indifferent the next also doesn't help. Find a way to hold but not squeeze. This allows them to be there when they want to be and not because they have to be.

# PISCES SUN/SCORPIO RISING

You wish you were as forgiving as Astrology books say. Every wound feels as fresh as the day it was inflicted and each insult still rings in your ears. Pisces people are capable of tremendous compassion and empathy. It's a natural quality that stems from being able to put yourself in somebody else's shoes. It's not hard to imagine how an absent or unloving parent could contribute to someone's cruelty or abusiveness. In fact, your own childhood may have included similar disappointments and betrayals, but you didn't turn out that way. You didn't become hard or cold. You extend your hand when it would be easier to keep it tucked inside your pocket.

Your Pisces Sun forgives, but your Scorpio Ascendant never forgets. You have sympathy for someone's history but that doesn't mean you'll revise it. You insist that everyone be held accountable for the harm they cause and the best way to do that is by making them experience firsthand the consequences of the pain they've inflicted on others. Pisces/Scorpio Risings are the avenging karmic angels of Astrology.

Now this doesn't mean that you'll spend your life stalking ex-bosses and heartless lovers. You're not going to disguise yourself, win their trust, and then bring about their ruin like Lisbeth Salander from *The Girl with the Dragon Tattoo*. But that won't prevent you from writing about it. Or singing about it. Or advocating against it socially or politically. When you're a Pisces/Scorpio Rising you feel people's pain on a molecular level and the only way to exorcise it is through some kind of creative or transformative process. Your Scorpio Rising never averts its gaze from the wrongs that can never be righted. It gives you purpose. And your Pisces Sun takes that raw material and turns it into a star performance, a number one hit, or a hashtag movement that speaks to millions. It's hurt made to heal.

But you can get a little too swept up in the righteous struggle, which is why you want to make sure you don't turn into the very thing you're fighting against. Outrage will always be Scorpio Rising's drug of choice, which is why it's up to the Pisces Sun to remind it that the point is to find peace or else you're just pouring gasoline on a fire.

# ARIES SUN/SCORPIO RISING

It's always do or die with you. There's no such thing as a dry run, mock combat, or just fooling around. You don't hold back, nor do you expect the other side to. When you play, you play for keeps. What you gain with this double Mars combination—Mars rules both Aries and Scorpio—is hyper-focus, a killer instinct, and a no-holds-barred attitude that makes others think twice about locking horns with you. You can be quite intimidating when you want to be. What you lose, however, with Scorpio in the Ascendant is the good sportsmanship that comes with being an Aries. You don't approach an opponent to shake hands afterward; you check to make sure that they'll never be able to use their hands again.

This doesn't exactly win you friends, which is why you need to dial it down. And this isn't new information. People have been telling you this since kindergarten when you began tossing playmates off tricycles with the fury of an action hero commandeering a vehicle in the middle of a high-speed chase. It would be one thing if you just got worked up about things. Then you could seek anger-management counseling or redirect aggressive impulses by taking martial arts classes. But when you've got as much Mars energy coursing through your horoscope as you do then the drive is to win at all costs. And this isn't exclusive to athletics. You might pursue a love interest with the precision tracking of a special ops unit or take out a rival at work by any means necessary. And again this isn't because you're malicious or mean-spirited. It's because you need to be on top.

Loved ones understand this. They've been pushed around, talked over, and shoved to one side enough times to get that this is just your nature. They also know that once the fury's spent you're full of remorse and will go to great lengths to make it up to them. However, it's still up to you to do something about you.

Ruling your passions doesn't mean overriding them. It means maintaining a grip on the runaway horses so that you're driving the chariot and not being trampled beneath its wheels. It also means less apologizing in the future, which is good because apologies have never been your strong suit.

# TAURUS SUN/SCORPIO RISING

You have a hard time believing that you're a vindictive person. You see yourself as kind and gentle. Or at least you would be if people would stop trying to mess with your things. Are you really supposed to stand idly by while they eye your possessions, drive a wedge between you and a loved one, or plot to bring you down at work? You have a right to defend yourself and to protect your interests. And you will by making haters, competitors, and two-faced friends rue the day they ever crossed you. You don't start fights but you will end them. And once you beat back the enemy, then things can go back to the way they once were—that is, until someone else tries to horn in on your turf.

You have this reputation for creating your own self-fulfilling prophecies. Forever suspicious of others' motives, you make it impossible for anyone to win your trust. You're the type who picks up the blank tile that someone just used to spell out a high-scoring word in Scrabble to make sure that it's not a letter tile flipped upside down. And it doesn't matter if it's always blank. The fact of the matter is one day it might not be and until then you will keep checking to see. Loved ones and friends got used to this a long time ago and find it strangely endearing. First dates? Not so much. There have been several times when they've excused themselves to go to the bathroom and never returned.

You really do see yourself as uncomplicated. And as long as people behave themselves then things don't have to get weird. Unfortunately, what happens with this kind of thinking is that you put the responsibility on others to behave while exonerating yourself, and this just isn't going to work in a relationship. Life is a two-way street and nowhere is that more emphasized than when your Sun is opposite your Ascendant. You can't just blame people for making you react the way you do. That's on you.

Your Scorpio Rising will stand down if you tell it to. And over time, as you learn that not everyone is out to get you or looking to pull a fast one, then you really will mellow out and relax.

# GEMINI SUN/SCORPIO RISING

For you, a mystery is a riddle that hasn't been solved yet. There's nothing so obscure, abstract, or supernatural that it can't be explained. But this doesn't make you a know-it-all. If anything, you'll go to great lengths to keep an open mind. Nothing skews a calculation or distorts a diagnosis like a hastily formed conclusion. You put your faith in your tools and in your process. If you come up with the wrong answer you won't try to make it fit like a square peg forced into a round hole. You'll retrace your steps—searching for the inconsistency you missed but know is there. No one works harder to get things right. And once you're ready to make your case it's airtight and utterly irrefutable.

Gemini/Scorpio Risings like to get to the bottom of what ails and fix it. Your professions range from mathematics to psychology, from investigative reporter to food critic. Gemini is ruled by Mercury, the messenger of the gods. Herald of Jupiter, only Mercury could travel from heaven to earth to hell and back again. There was no place he couldn't go. And in the same vein you are driven to consider every scenario, explore every avenue, and exhaust every resource in your pursuit of the truth. It's your Scorpio Rising that directs you to sniff out those secret places that people overlook. You don't think twice about asking deeply personal questions or raising taboo topics.

One would think you'd be more sensitive given the delicate terrain you trod, but you can sometimes be quite caustic. You don't mean to be biting. It comes from the pressure you put on yourself. Stress is something you need to take seriously. The fact that you demand so much of yourself mentally can lead to too much coffee in the morning and too much alcohol at night. The other thing to watch out for is weaponizing words. Geminis are naturally flippant but your Scorpio Rising can turn a jab into a stab. You need to monitor this when you're feeling exhausted because that's when you let the barbs fly. It doesn't matter how brilliant your mind is if nobody wants to listen to what you have to say. There's no harm in taking the extra time to soften your remarks. People will respect you even more.

# CANCER SUN/SCORPIO RISING

One would think you were enrolled in the United States Witness Security Program the way you duck out of having your picture taken. You don't do social media, rarely give out your mailing address, and will spend hours manufacturing aliases and fictional biographies to go along with them. People never come to you. You go to them—materializing out of thin air and vanishing just as mysteriously when the appointment's over or the hookup has finished. You delight in misleading others and keeping them guessing, which is ironic for someone who's as sentimental and folksy as you.

Cancers are nurturing and affectionate. You happily spoil the people you care about and won't think twice about sacrificing your welfare for theirs. Your dream is to find the perfect mate who gets you and to spend the rest of your life together raising puppies, crops, and maybe even children. Unfortunately there's a catch. There always is when you're a Scorpio

Rising. Maybe it's the emotional baggage, the psychological scarring, or a sordid past. Whatever it is, it's serious and that's what creates this feeling of being on the run.

Thankfully it's your inner demons and not actual people who are chasing you, but that doesn't make it much easier. No two signs are as self-reflective as Cancer and Scorpio. You have spent more time plumbing the depths and facing your fears than any other constellation in the zodiac. But that only makes you more secretive and guarded. Instead of divulging what's going on, you'll disguise your anxieties by portraying yourself as worry-free. And people, being people, will happily accept things at face value.

There's a part of you that wants to be found out. It's why you're always dropping hints or leaving behind clues, but it needs to be the right person who does the finding. Someone who's as canny, compulsive, and as unknowable as you. But what makes for great erotic fiction doesn't always translate to day-to-day life. At some point you need to come out of hiding and show your true face to the world. It may seem like you're giving away the mystery that makes you special, but what you're really doing is trading a spectral existence for a more substantive one.

## LEO SUN/SCORPIO RISING

There's an exceptionalism built into Leos born around noon. This is when the Sun is at the highest point in the horoscope, which means that you are used to looking down on people. And it's not because you're conceited or full of yourself. It's more like the difference between living in a penthouse apartment versus a basement studio. You get more light, have all kinds of space, and nobody's going to be peeping through your street-level window. You are above it all. Your blazing Sun can't help but call attention to itself. It comes with having good looks, a standout talent, or astonishingly good fortune. Used to being admired, praised, and even studied, you accepted long ago that your life is on show 24/7.

Your Scorpio Rising can taste the envy in the room. It knows better than to lower its guard. It understands that most people want to be friends because you have something they don't. Suspicious and skeptical, it could be said that your Ascendant acts as your bodyguard as it studies people's faces, assesses their characters, and introduces test questions aimed at exposing the inconsistencies in their story. All of this is done in a genial manner. The fact that most everyone believes it only proves that you were right about them all along.

Your weak spot is your heart. When you fall for someone, you fall BIG— and it's almost never the person everyone expected it to be. They were picturing you with someone glamorous and untouchable. What they weren't counting on was a diamond in the rough. And this is where your Scorpio Rising plays a more powerful role than your Leo Sun because it can smell a soul mate even if the packaging is all wrong. What follows is you trying to convince this person that you belong together. It's ironic how you can effortlessly capture the heart of everyone but the person you're attracted to most. This is the one area of your life where you are humbled time and again. It's never pleasant, but it's good for the soul. Pluto, the ruler of Scorpio, is the planet of ordeals and the transformations that arise from them. It says you can't get what you want without going through hell first. Thankfully Pluto also rewards those who brave its trials.

# VIRGO SUN/SCORPIO RISING

You're the one who drinks sparkling water while everyone else parties. And it doesn't matter if it's a dance club, a family wedding, or Burning Man—it is your natural inclination to abstain. You prefer to be clearheaded than under the influence. But you don't come across as prudish or judgmental. On the contrary, you blend in perfectly. You can follow the meandering threads of conversation, help out with the jokes when the teller forgets the punch line, and even walk revelers to the bathroom if they've had too much to drink. People feel comfortable handing you their car keys, phones, and sometimes clothes. They know that they're safe in your hands. This same trustworthiness applies to work. Supervisors, co-workers, and even clients are always seeking you out for those off-the-record conversations.

Virgos are famously critical, but you rarely show it if you're a Virgo/Scorpio Rising. That's because the quickest way to ensure someone's non-cooperation is to get on their case. Instead you'll go ahead and implement the things you think should be done by planting seeds. You learned a long time ago the value of sprinkling a trail of breadcrumbs that leads to the conclusion you want someone to make. Moreover, if you can make them feel like they were the ones who came up with the idea in the first place then it's all the better. One might say you're being manipulative, but it's OK because it's for a good cause.

No one has ever seen you lose your shit. And it's unlikely they ever will. You are a master at deflecting the conversation away from you and onto others' problems. And if there's anything people want to talk about it's their problems. However, the one who has seen you lose it is the one who turned you down. That's the person who said they weren't ready for a commitment or decided you were better off as friends. This is the one you bad-mouthed and turned others against; the person who experienced your vindictiveness and still remained cordial. Your biggest guilty secret.

Virgo/Scorpio Risings are social creatures despite your longing to be left alone. It's important for you to be exposed to fresh takes on things—otherwise you become stuffy and pedantic. Debates, arguments, and in-depth discussions are good for the mind and soul. As is the occasional meltdown.

# LIBRA SUN/SCORPIO RISING

Why is it that you only get together with people when they're going through a crisis? And when the crisis is over they move on—without so much as a thank-you? It's amazing how you can be innocently flirting with someone in line at Starbucks and within moments you'll learn about their lopsided relationship, loveless marriage, or parent who's in hospice care. Then again, they may be harboring a big secret and you're the first person they came clean to. Now this should be a signal to turn around and walk away as fast as you can—and if you were a Libra born at any other time of day you would—but you know that by the time you pay for your lattes you'll be hooked. For some people it's a glance. For others it's a smile. But for you it's the secret and once shared it ties you to that person tighter than a hundred past lives in ancient Egypt ever could.

Libra/Scorpio Rising is probably one of the most challenging Sun Sign/Rising Sign combinations in Astrology—and it's not because of the signs, but rather the part of the sky that was rising when you were born. It's called "Via Combusta," or "Fiery Road." The energies of both malefic influences are magnified here—Mars because it rules your Scorpio Ascendant and Saturn because of its association with the house where your Sun resides. Translation? You couldn't avoid these emotional car wrecks if you tried. And it's not because you suffer from low self-esteem or are a born masochist who forgot their safe word. It's because these encounters make your heart grow by breaking it.

So is your love life a patch of scorched earth from start to finish? No. If anything, it's just the opposite. It makes you more compassionate and streetwise. Repeated heartbreaks deepen the wisdom *and* the humor by turning you into a breath of fresh air in others' Sturm und Drang. And when you do find the right mate—and you will because this is what it's all about—it won't be someone who leaves you at the curb after you've been there for them. It will be someone who's lived a life similar to yours and gets where you're coming from. Someone who recognizes that you were made for each other.

# SAGITTARIUS RISING

How could anyone miss you? You're the loudest voice in the room. You're the one telling the most off-color story, throwing your head back

**You're the loudest voice in the room.**

in laughter, or outshouting the person you're arguing with. And even if you're not especially vocal, you're still *loud*—like with that tie you've got on, the smile you flash, or the makeup you wear. You learned a long time ago to stop hiding your light under a bushel because it's just going to shine through no matter what you do. Your spirit is irrepressible—and you've got a long history of time-outs, public scenes, and professional reprimands to prove it. Nobody's done more time in the doghouse than you have.

Yet people always respond to you affectionately. It's amazing what they'll forgive and how many times they'll forgive it. And it's not because you're a fast talker or have them under your spell. It's because you genuinely mean well. Yes, you'll bumble this, trip over that, and often show up late for important functions, but you are so effusively apologetic and sad-eyed in your remorse that loved ones and friends can't help but welcome you back into their arms. It's like trying to stay mad at a favorite cartoon character.

There's a casualness to Sagittarius Rising and a fearlessness too. It comes from the fact that Jupiter is Sagittarius's Ruling Planet. Jupiter was the king of the gods in Roman mythology. Everyone knew to bow down to him. However, Jupiter hated the pomp and circumstance of the heavenly court, which is why he was always sneaking off down to earth to gallivant with the human folk. He preferred the company of mortals to the snobbery of the gods, which is why you can speak truth to people in power in the same easygoing manner that you'll chat with the Lyft driver about her workday. Everyone's equal in your eyes—except for you, of course. Rules that apply to others never apply to you. You're just naturally exempt.

You're a screamer. All Sagittarius Risings are. It's the storm god in you. You can be talking in sweet dulcet tones one moment and then shrieking at the top of your lungs the next. But like a summer downpour it passes quickly and life soon returns to normal. Now you know there are no hard feelings and that you were just venting, but for some people your temper can be frightening—especially since the change in mood is so sudden and dramatic. Don't be insulted when they run for cover and be sure to give them plenty of time to reappear when they're ready.

# SAGITTARIUS SUN/SAGITTARIUS RISING

People turn to you for moral support. They know that no matter how bad they feel you can cheer them up. Your concern is heartfelt, your optimism unflappable, and you've an endless supply of cheesy jokes that could bring a smile to any long face. It doesn't matter how dire the straits, you always look on the bright side. You have this uncanny ability to use a debacle as a teaching moment and explain how a situation *not* turning out as hoped may prove to be a godsend. At times your rationale seems far-fetched, but the point isn't for you to have all the answers to life's problems. It's to rekindle flagging spirits so that people get up on their feet and climb back on top of the horse that threw them.

Sometimes you can go overboard with the motivational speeches—like when you deliberately look for provocative things to say to get a rise out of someone. You think that pissing them off will show that there's still fight left in them but oftentimes it makes matters worse by rubbing salt in the wounds. You need to develop a fuller understanding of the different ways that people process their emotions. Some people love a colorful pep talk while others need to be left alone for a while. And just because they retreat to their tents doesn't mean that they've given up.

You take your beliefs seriously. Whether it's a religious faith, a spiritual path, or a self-help curriculum you will not be talked out of something you know to be true. And it doesn't matter how many arguments you get into. If anything, you welcome a full-throated debate. Nothing beats a good verbal food fight with stats, facts, quotes, and citations being thrown around indiscriminately. You're not invested in proving that what you believe is right. You already know it is. However, if you can convince a naysayer to come around to your way of seeing things then you will surely be vindicated.

No one will ever accuse you of being a cynic; however, accusations of gullibility sting. And that's because you're an easy mark for a good sob story. Your trusting nature will always be your weakness, but despite all the disappointments nothing can shake your faith in the miracle cure of a positive outlook.

# CAPRICORN SUN/SAGITTARIUS RISING

It's hard to believe that you're a Capricorn because you come across as such an upper, not a downer. There's a crackling enthusiasm that pops right out of you. When you start talking about something that excites you your eyes flash, your expressions grow more animated, and your voice practically booms across the room. People draw close, attracted by an exhilaration they find irresistible and secretly hope is infectious. You dream big, believe that anything is possible, and aren't shy about leading with your highest hopes. You're on fire!

Yet you are as Capricorn as they come. Born under Saturn, the planet of fear and inhibition, you don't feel like you're this person everyone sees and worry that they may have gotten the wrong impression. This is what happens when you're born in the hours just before Sunrise. People see the Rising Sign first and you second—if ever. This gets especially complicated when others find your horoscopic face so appealing. Who could blame you for wanting to play along?

It's easy letting people think what they want to think. They're happy to buy whatever you're selling and they're not too interested in disclaimers. However, being a Capricorn Sun, you live with this constant dread of being found out, waiting for the day when your lover realizes you're not the zippy person they fell in love with or an associate at work exposes you as a closet depressive. Yet that day has never come. And it never will. That's because your Rising Sign isn't some disguise that you put on like a false beard or a blond wig. It's you. It may not be a side of you that you recognize, but it's still you.

It's no secret that you're prone to dark moods. Loved ones and friends have known all along about your paralyzing self-doubt and how you will fret more over the few cents lost than the dollars gained. Yet they also know you always come back online again. At some point you will get inspired about a new venture or a proposition will seize your imagination and that low-burning flame will roar back to life. This may be something you'll never understand, but others do and that's how they can keep the faith going until you're ready to believe in yourself again.

# AQUARIUS SUN/SAGITTARIUS RISING

You are completely at home with people who are not at all like you. Maybe you grew up in a foreign country, moved around a lot as a child, or were shipped off to live with wealthy relatives, à la Will Smith in *The Fresh Prince of Bel-Air.* Where other horoscopes might have suffered from a lack of roots and feeling of "otherness," you wound up doing the opposite. You thrived! That's because few Rising Signs are as outgoing as Sagittarius and to be born under an Aquarius Sun means that you have an open-minded approach to any social situation you're thrown into. There's no such thing as a stranger as far as you're concerned, just a friend you haven't met yet.

It's hard for people to take you at face value. Are you really this easygoing? Ironically it's your guilelessness that makes them uncomfortable. They have a difficult time believing that you're not putting on an act or trying to pull the wool over their eyes. You aren't. At least not consciously, but affability should never be mistaken for accommodating or long-suffering. You're still a Sagittarius Rising. You'll hop atop your soapbox without blinking should the occasion arise, and your Aquarius Sun has never been shy about airing radical opinions or views.

You believe that everyone deserves a seat at the table. You also believe that they should be polite about it. All air signs are concerned with proper etiquette and your Aquarius Sun is no different. Often portrayed as rebellious, you're never unruly. Aquarians are famously committed to making sure that every voice is heard. This is augmented by your Sagittarius Rising, which is hospitable and welcoming by nature. The idea of breaking bread with others—especially those who don't see eye to eye with you—is a core value. Looking for common ground in our humanity while celebrating its diversity is your mission statement.

Aquarius Suns with Sagittarius Rising gravitate toward social work and community organizing. There's a strong sense of civic responsibility and moral purpose. There can also be a penchant for proselytizing. And it doesn't matter what you're on a soapbox about, Aquarius Sun/Sagittarius Risings often pop up on street corners handing out pamphlets with the bright-eyed perkiness of a flight attendant passing out pretzels and biscotti cookies.

# PISCES SUN/SAGITTARIUS RISING

Yours is what they call an "artistic temperament." And you don't have to be a painter or musician to possess it. Your highs are so breathlessly transcendent and your lows so profoundly abysmal that there can be no middle ground. Some may find it dizzying the way that you laugh through your tears and sigh longingly with every triumph, but that's only because they're incapable of appreciating the full spectrum of your psychic palette. Like the mysterious realm your Ruling Planet Neptune is named for, you experience emotions most people haven't even discovered, much less knew existed. And your Pisces Sun is more than happy to keep those hidden depths hidden.

But that's not how your Rising Sign works. Sagittarius is a fire sign—public and demonstrative. Everything needs to be out in the open with you. That's why you'll keep knocking until the door opens, weigh in on conversations taking place at neighboring tables, and are the first to start sharing in group therapy. It's your job to get people talking about those sides of themselves they want to sweep under the rug. You inspire them to draw upon their inner truths so that they can live more fully realized lives. Is it any wonder that Pisces Suns with Sagittarius Rising want to be pastors, gurus, and acting coaches?

Your attraction to others' struggles holds out hope for learning to cope with your own highs and lows. And they are literally highs and lows. Your Rising Sign is ruled by Jupiter—named after the Roman god of the sky—and your Sun Sign is ruled by Neptune—named after the Roman god of the sea. At first the differences seem irreconcilable, until you remember that oceans are the wellspring of clouds. Clouds form from evaporated water. And when clouds grow heavy, they rain, pouring their water back into the sea. This ongoing partnership between sky and water reflects the cyclical relationship between your Sun Sign and Rising Sign. Each sustains the other.

Once you accept that highs and lows are just your psyche's way of inhaling and exhaling, you'll feel less crazy. You may still have trouble explaining away your tempestuous personality—but then what else do you expect from a Sun Sign/Rising Sign combination ruled by two storm gods?

# ARIES SUN/SAGITTARIUS RISING

You're never around. Always away on a business trip or tour of duty, you come home just long enough to do some laundry, repack your bags, and set off again. You spend a lot of time apart from the people you care about. One would think they don't matter, but nothing could be further from the truth. Some zodiac signs stick close to home, dreaming of the world beyond their backyard fence, while others live out of a suitcase, longing for the time when they can be reunited with their loved ones. You're one of them.

*Wanderlust* is a word often used with your Rising Sign. That's because Sagittarius is famous for falling in love with distant lands and then booking the next flight out. However, your Sun Sign rarely does anything on a lark. There are usually extenuating circumstances. Maybe you can't do what you do for a living if you stayed put, opportunities may be scarce in your native country and it's your job to send money back home, or the culture you were raised in frowns on people like you. There's often a feeling of self-exile woven into the horoscope of an Aries Sun/Sagittarius Rising. Then again, your Aries Sun may be drawn to a career in the military, sports, or entertainment—professions famous for their demanding travel schedules.

You're like a kid in a candy store when it comes to matters of the heart. It's impossible to have just one. Actually, what you're looking for is *the one*, but you keep discovering someone sweeter, creamier, and more delicious. You don't mean to be unfaithful. Ironically you're one of the few signs who's completely honest about your feelings. When you're in love, you're in love. And when you're not? Then it's over.

Aries Sun/Sagittarius Risings resist settling down. You're afraid the moment you do your fire will be snuffed out. And that might be true. There's a reason why medieval knights went on decades-long quests searching for holy grails or fire-breathing dragons. It was all about the adventure. Once you realize that love is its own adventure—every bit as enchanting and enriching as an epic journey—then you'll be OK with coming home again. You might even unpack and stick around awhile.

# TAURUS SUN/SAGITTARIUS RISING

You were born without a filter. Easily irritated and totally vocal about it, you'll call attention to everyday infractions and transgressions whenever you experience them. You're the person most likely to start clapping when a glass shatters in a restaurant, to bang on the hood of a car stuck in the crosswalk, or ask if anyone else smells something funny in a tightly packed elevator. People may look at you disapprovingly, but you'll only roll your eyes. Why should you act like nothing's happened when everybody knows it has?

Taurus Suns are known for their thick skins, but not when you have Sagittarius Rising. The least little thing sets you off. It's like your senses have been amplified—especially taste and smell. You can tell the difference in quality and grade right away. Where most zodiac signs avoid wanting to make trouble, you won't think twice about insisting the mechanic go back over what he's just done until he's uncovered the problem you know is still there. When something doesn't feel right with you, then it's not right. And usually you are one hundred percent on target. It's why you won't stop until what's amiss has been remedied.

Now nobody has a problem with you being a perfectionist. If anything, they marvel that you're better informed than most experts. That's because you enjoy research and will even research for research's sake. It's just that your bedside manner can be a bit gruff. You can come across as bellicose, demanding, and even reveling in someone else's mistake. And this is something you might want to take a look at.

It's because of the placement of the Sun in your horoscope that you're convinced people aren't listening to you. Born when the Sun had just set, you're hounded by this feeling of something having been forgotten or left out and everyone being OK with it. This prompts your Sagittarius Rising to leap into action and sound the alarm—again and again.

You need to trust that people got the message the first time. You're a very big presence and nobody's going to overlook you. What you want to do, however, is exercise your authority confidently. People who are confident in themselves only say what they have to say once. And if someone doesn't listen? Then it's on them, not you.

## GEMINI SUN/SAGITTARIUS RISING

If your friends told you to jump off a bridge, would you? Yes. But not because you do whatever your friends say. You'd do it because they don't think you'd dare. When you're a Gemini Sun with Sagittarius Rising you love to thrill and astonish like a circus aerialist spinning above the heads of the crowd. The more outrageous the challenge, the faster you'll accept it. People think you're reckless, but you're not. You just know you've got a guardian angel looking out for you.

Sagittarius Risings have a wide-eyed trust in Providence. It's why you take cannonball dives into the unknown—especially in personal and professional relationships. You're the first one to say "I love you," finalize a contract without reviewing the fine print, or hire someone on the spot because they have a trustworthy face. You have this unshakable faith that everything in life happens for a reason and if things don't turn out the way you expect, then it will still somehow work out in the end.

Needless to say, this isn't the way your Gemini Sun views things. If anything, it's horrified by the way you'll happily sign away your rights in a burst of magnanimity or agree to less money because the other person needs it more than you. But when you're born at Sunset like you were then it's the Rising Sign that's behind the wheel of your horoscope and the Sun Sign that's in the passenger seat. That's because the Sun was decreasing in light and strength while the Rising Sign was growing into it. Think of Jiminy Cricket and Pinocchio. Your Gemini Sun can tug at your conscience all it likes, but your Sagittarius Rising will race ahead undeterred because who wants to listen to a nag?

You've made plenty of mistakes and probably have the divorce settlements and lawsuits to prove it. But mistakes aren't strikes against you. They're signs of a life well lived. There's no such thing as heartbreak, business failure, or betrayal as long as you gained something from the experience. Maybe it was that once-in-a-lifetime love, those twelve years when you were riding high, or the chance to show that you were the better person when it mattered. Everybody makes mistakes, but how many can boast of having no regrets?

# CANCER SUN/SAGITTARIUS RISING

You possess the healing touch. Instinctively reaching out to hold a lonely hand or wrapping a supportive arm around heartbroken shoulders, you have an ease and grace around people who have been dealt a harsh blow by life. You're not frightened by misfortune. You've done as much time on top of the heap looking down as you have at the bottom of the barrel looking up, and others can sense that immediately. It gives you a gravitas, a sort of street cred. The blessing to being born under Cancer, a zodiac sign that's ruled by the Moon, is an inherent feel for when fortunes wax and wane. You can take the booms with the busts.

Your Sagittarius Rising provides you with a halo of protection. Although you've suffered hardship and pain, your Rising Sign confers a robust psychic immune system able to shake off any ill effects. It's why you have no qualms about sitting down with those others shun, broaching taboo subjects nobody wants to talk about, or coaxing the most die-hard misers into opening their wallets for a good cause. If anyone can get water from a stone, it's you. Cancer Suns with Sagittarius Risings are Astrology's Good Samaritans. You're just as likely to show up bedside at the ICU as you are at a gala dinner, fundraising for a philanthropic institution.

Yet you can be hard to know—even to yourself. There are so many layers to your personality and you're not exactly consistent. Caught in the crosscurrents of a boisterous Ascendant and a nurturing Sun Sign, people are surprised to discover a submissive side. This comes out in romantic relationships. There's something about your horoscope that keeps pairing you with partners you're financially beholden to. Either they *make* more money, which leaves you feeling resentful and like you're under their thumb, or they *owe* more money, which means you're constantly bankrolling them in hopes that one day their luck will change.

It takes several years to figure out the right design for living. Mostly because you want your home and your independence too. You may have to go through a couple of marriages and move back and forth from the city to the country, but once you work out the proper fit, then everything falls into place.

# LEO SUN/SAGITTARIUS RISING

Your face lights up immediately when your name is called. Gifted with a cheerful expression and a beaming aura, you really are a joy to behold. You could enter a room wearing a barrel with a lampshade over your head and people would still know it's you. Yours is one of the few Sun Sign/Rising Sign combinations where it doesn't much matter what you look like, whom you know, or how you dress. Everyone wants to bask in your company. They know there's something about you that's heaven-sent and if only they could get close enough then some of what you have might find its way to them.

Fortune smiles on you when you have Sagittarius Rising, but it's especially doting if you're a Leo. You're Astrology's trust-fund baby. Closed doors open at the touch, opportunities tumble into your lap, and you're at the right place at the right time so often that it might as well be a bus stop. It's a nice problem to have until others start looking at you like the goose who laid the golden egg. It's one thing to deal with people who covet what you have; it's quite another problem when what they covet is you. It's something to watch out for in your romantic relationships, but also be wary of it with supervisors and bosses. Their lack of praise has nothing to do with your job performance; it's aimed at keeping you down. People don't want to let you go when you're a Leo Sun with Sagittarius Rising. They know a good thing when they see it.

Unfortunately, there's no avoiding the pitfalls of falling for jealous types, being manipulated by rivals, and cheated by money managers, but like the Sun, which is your Ruling Planet, you will always rise on a new day. Moreover, your Sagittarius Ascendant ensures that you'll emerge the wiser and better for it.

Steer clear of behind-the-scenes shenanigans or under-the-table wheeling and dealing. When you command the spotlight like you do then whatever happens—no matter how discreetly handled—will always be found out. And it won't be pretty. It's kind of like driving a red car. Lots of people can speed on the freeway and get away with it, but you'll be the one that the cops pull over.

## VIRGO SUN/SAGITTARIUS RISING

You can fire off zingers with the hawkeyed accuracy of a William Tell shooting an apple off his kid's head. Your quips, comebacks, and subtle innuendos always hit their mark, which is why people learned a long time ago not to mess with you. Everyone knows that you're wickedly smart and dangerously funny, yet you never come across as mean-spirited. You get close, but you stop short.

Precocious from birth, you quickly rose through the ranks at school.

Once you figured out what was expected of you, it was easy to master the curriculum, fly through tests, and walk away with all the prizes. You would have spent your entire youth branded as a teacher's pet if it weren't for your Rising Sign's penchant for making trouble. It has a sixth sense for where the fun is and it's not in math club. Flamboyant, wild, and adventurous, you have your Sagittarius Rising to thank for never becoming a know-it-all or turning into a prude.

But not even your devil-may-care Ascendant can divert you from your relentless pursuit of excellence. Your Virgo Sun—prominently featured at the top of your Astrology chart—outshines everything else. Most people see their Best Self as something to aspire to, a higher standard of being infused with spiritual purpose and moral integrity. You see your Best Self as something out of reach. Like a Sisyphean labor, it's a contest you can't win but can't walk away from either. As long as you can conceive of something better any accomplishment is a near miss.

Everyone knows that Virgos can be impossibly critical and never more than with themselves. It comes from having a mind that's steps ahead of everyone else's and that eagerly ferrets out defects and inconsistencies. Living with a mind like this isn't easy because, though brilliant, it can also become paralyzing with its fixation on details, technicalities, and exhaustive cataloguing of everything that should have been done but wasn't. The beauty of a Sagittarius Rising is in its resistance to coloring inside the lines. It's always looking for ways to test limits, buck the system, and run free. Find a way to harness its creative energy and you'll never become penned in and formulaic. Moreover, you'll ensure that the horse remains in front of the cart instead of the other way around.

# LIBRA SUN/SAGITTARIUS RISING

You have this way of making someone feel like the most brilliant person in the room. You hang on their every word, laugh at all their jokes, and know just the follow-up question to ask to keep them engaged. You're an expert conversationalist because you are genuinely interested in people's takes on things. And it doesn't much matter if you're hobnobbing with Kim Kardashian or the CEO of a cement mixing company, you will inevitably touch upon a topic they're truly passionate about. Maybe it's their outlook on life, hopes for the future, or concerns about the direction the world is heading. It's amazing how even the most taciturn type will open up about philosophical matters they don't usually discuss. That's why you're the person everyone wants to sit next to at the dinner party.

Libra Suns are typically beautiful and unassuming. Tasteful and elegant, you prefer to be the jewelry, not the person wearing it. You'll often appear on the arm of someone who's important but could use a boost in the looks department. You know that you were born to adorn.

However, all of this changes when you have Sagittarius on the Ascendant. Famous for their love of extravagance and unapologetic bling, Libra/Sagittarius Risings want to make a dazzling first impression—jaw-dropping and unforgettable. But sometimes you can get carried away. That's why it always pays to take a look in the mirror and remove at least three to five accessories before leaving the house. You don't want to come across as fashion's version of the neighbor at Christmastime who has twenty Nativity scenes and a herd of Santa sleighs pulled by eight tiny reindeer on their front lawn.

The biggest challenge for a Libra/Sagittarius Rising is trusting in your power of attraction. You don't have to body tackle a love interest, wow the boss, or lasso a potential client and wrestle them to the ground. They will inevitably come to you on their own. Admittedly *wait and see* isn't programmed into your Rising Sign's DNA—you like to target prospects and gallop off in hot pursuit—but give it a try. Not only will you wind up surrounded by friends in high places who can open doors for you, but they'll happily introduce you to their friends who can do even more.

## SCORPIO SUN/SAGITTARIUS RISING

When you smile, you smile with your heart *and* soul. It beams like a break in the cloud cover or the early morning sun when it peers over the mountains. It's so promising that people can't help but turn in your direction. Everything about it is trustworthy. Your smile is so honest that it's immediately apparent when your mood has changed. A shadow falls across your face. It's ironic that for a zodiac sign famous for keeping secrets, your Sagittarius Rising always gives you away.

Scorpios are brutally honest. It's why you're not exactly forthcoming when asked to weigh in with what you really think. You'll take a long time to answer as you work out how much of the truth you think the other person can handle. But truth takes on a more redemptive purpose when you have Sagittarius Rising. Truth is meant to save, not humiliate. That's why the truth you speak doesn't come from a holy book or an esoteric philosophy. It's a personal truth, one embedded in a history that's not always pretty. It comes from all the times you poisoned a well, jealously withheld something from someone more deserving, or profited at another's expense. Some people can get away with things like this, but not you. When your Ruling Planet is Pluto, named after the Roman god of the dead, you are judged for your actions in this lifetime, not the next. And those actions will come back to haunt you until you make things right.

You're determined to live a good life. Not one absorbed in mea culpas, but a life devoted to lifting people up. You might help them face problems you yourself have faced or be an agent of justice in their lives. Then again your personal truth might touch others through your artwork, photography, or writing—creative expressions that resonate on a deep level.

Every Scorpio knows what it's like to descend into the dark night of the soul, but when you're a Scorpio with Sagittarius Rising you're more interested in the morning after. Sagittarius is a sign that will slog through the worst that life has to throw at it as long as there's a moral to the story or a lesson to be learned. It's your job to share that journey with the rest of us.

# CAPRICORN RISING

You're famous for shaking your head no and saying things will never work with an Eeyore-like finality. You're dour and a tad gloomy, and people know better than to argue **You know your stuff.** with you. And it's not because you're a downer (although you can be); it's because you're right. You know your stuff. Never one to answer quickly or to act in the moment, anything deemed worthy of your attention is given the utmost scrutiny. You'll review the latest studies, research a subject with the categorical thoroughness of an archaeological dig, and ask the questions nobody else thought to ask. It's true that you have a reputation for poking holes in people's dreams and deflating their fondest hopes, but it's in service to disabusing them of any foolish notions. In a world where everyone is pushing the pedal to the metal, you have the unenviable task of riding the brake. You got used to taking the heat for it a long time ago.

Even as a baby, you had a serious face. That's why loved ones would try to get you to smile and giggle by squeezing your feet or playing peekaboo, but one look from you was all it took to make them stop. And that look is famous to this day. Maybe it's an arched eyebrow, a withering side glance, or a dull expression of boredom. You may never win any popularity contests, but you're instantly recognizable to the select few who share your sardonic view of the world. It's an exclusive group and one you're proud to be a member of.

Saturn, the planet of time, rules Capricorn. That's why you look the same from decade to decade. Others may grow wrinkled and gray, but you would be instantly recognizable at your fiftieth high school reunion. When people say you haven't aged a day, they mean it. Subsequently you do much better in your later years than your younger ones. It's a bit of a tall order— having to watch others succeed and flourish while you negotiate the long detours and delays that are part of Saturn's curriculum, but once you get into your forties things begin to come together for you. It's slow at first, but you can definitely feel the change, so the result is that you wind up cele-brating your accomplishments at a time in life when you can truly appreci-ate them while everyone else reminisces about their peak years gone by. Being a Capricorn Rising is akin to a bottle of fine wine. Open it too early and its taste is unremarkable; drink it after it's been properly aged and the experience proves worth the wait.

## CAPRICORN SUN/CAPRICORN RISING

If somebody handed you an opportunity on a silver platter—like a big break, a valuable introduction, or the keys to your own Jaguar—you'd probably hand it back. And it's not because you're being difficult or un-grateful. You just don't like it when people do you favors. It makes you un-comfortable. You don't want to feel indebted to anyone for anything. It's why you pay your own way, never ask for a helping hand, and beg off when it comes to exchanging gifts. This can create the impression of making things harder for yourself than need be, but that's only because you want to show the world that you're not a taker. Dignity means a lot to you.

Capricorns think about money constantly. People assume it's because they're misers, but actually it's because you were born under Saturn, the planet of trials and tribulations. You know what it's like to do without. Either you came from nothing or your family experienced a financial setback when you were young. Capricorn/Capricorn Risings are no strangers to hardship. It marks you for life. Now, you may think tough times have made you resourceful—a rugged individualist who knows how to take care of yourself—but it's damaged you as well. Tough times have made you put up walls.

It's difficult going through life with your guard up. At a certain point people stop trying to get through to you and simply take you at face value. It's more convenient that way. If you don't want the song "All By Myself" to become a self-fulfilling prophecy, then you're going to have to learn how to lower those deflector shields and open hailing frequencies. Capricorn/Capricorn Risings can be so afraid of losing that they never let themselves win. Testing people without knowing what the answers are or holding back instead of expressing what you feel isn't exactly conducive to a well-lived life. Most horoscopes harden over time, but yours is meant to soften. Believe people when they say that they're at a loss as to how to get close to you. One of the big lessons for you to learn is that interdependency is the stuff of relationships. You can't have intimacy without it. After all— wouldn't you rather hug a person than a cactus?

# AQUARIUS SUN/CAPRICORN RISING

There's something about your delivery that leaves people wondering if you really believe in what you say. Maybe it's the tense chuckle, the forced smile, or the visible sign of relief when you finally get what you want. They don't understand how stressful it is for you to make a simple request nor can they fathom why—after having gotten what you wanted—you would start listing all the obstacles that still remain and things that could go horribly wrong. It's a nervous reaction on your part because you feel under pressure and you don't want to disappoint, but people don't always see that. Instead, your anxiety unwittingly creates the impression that nothing makes you happy.

Saturn rules Capricorn and Aquarius. And in true Saturnine fashion, both signs tend to focus on faults. Capricorn focuses on what's missing and Aquarius focuses on where things fell short. Together they exhibit an intolerance toward accepting anything *less than*—as evidenced in your despondent sighs and pained expressions. Disappointment is hardwired into all the wintry signs. Now usually a Capricorn Rising would keep their reservations quiet, but Aquarius is an air sign, which means that your thinking is done out loud. You feel like it's important to be transparent. It shows honesty and integrity. Others regard it as TMI. They just want to enjoy the sausage. They aren't really interested in how it gets made.

It takes a while for Aquarius/Capricorn Risings to realize that they're wearing their clothes inside out, but once they do then everything gets sorted out quickly. No longer prone to issuing apologies and disclaimers, you take ownership of your actions. This often coincides with a time in your life (after forty) when you go from follower to leader. Aquarius/Capricorn Risings don't like to think of themselves as the person in charge—it feels like you're somehow being set up for failure, but in truth nobody does it better. Your ability to read the big picture, to push forward and make the decisions nobody wants to make proves you're a natural executive. Plus, you'll relax once you have your hands on the steering wheel. You may not make the big revolutionary changes everyone expects from an Aquarius, but you'll find a way to make the ones that matter work. Your Capricorn Rising guarantees it.

# PISCES SUN/CAPRICORN RISING

You have a poet's patience for finding the right words. They need to be simple, precise, and resonant. You don't say anything off the cuff or haphazardly. A conversation isn't a blank page asking to be filled with scribbles. It's something you take seriously, more seriously than most. That's why you sound so bookish when you speak; not academic, but bookish in the well-read way that your sentences flow together like finely crafted prose. This is why people listen to you so intently. They literally hang on your every word. Everything you communicate is done with careful thought and an eye on how you would like things to play out in the end.

Pisces cleans up well when paired with Capricorn Rising. No faraway looks, disheveled appearance, or history of disappearing acts. Pisces/Capricorn Risings are perfectly prompt, polished, and present. Because you're famously reliable and responsible, people lean on you with little idea of what's going on inside. To be born under Pisces means that you are no stranger to pain and sorrow. It is the nature of your sign to suffer, just like it's the nature of Capricorn to cover it up. No one ever suspects how deeply wounded you are—not even close friends and intimates. They don't intuit silences like you do or share your ability to read between the lines. They assume that you're as calm as your sedate expression and as certain as your matter-of-fact air.

Your confidence that loved ones know how much you value them is misplaced. In your efforts to never show weakness or fallibility you can come across as not needing anyone. This is reinforced by the display of your considerable talents. You're very good at redirecting a conversation, leading others to the conclusions you wanted them to make, and even creating the impression that something special was shared when it really wasn't. You play your cards close to your chest. You know what you're holding in your hands and have a pretty good idea of what others are holding in theirs. Yet none of this is shared in the way that it needs to be if you want people to stick around.

No one's expecting you to unburden your soul, but a glimpse into its inner workings would help. People need to feel needed. You, more than anyone, know that.

## ARIES SUN/CAPRICORN RISING

It's hard to tell if it's the sneer or the smirk that gives you away first. You're not shy about broadcasting your disdain for people who think they're better than you. Indeed, you will go out of your way to take them down a peg—even if they never did you any harm. The sworn enemy of pretentious experts who flaunt their credentials and the privileged elite who were installed in positions they never earned, you can be unrelenting in your mission to expose, debunk, and even beat them at their own game. It's ironic that it's the people you say you can't abide who unwittingly push you to be better than you could ever be on your own. Maybe it's competition, maybe it's envy, but that mix of Mars and Saturn energies refuses to give up or give in.

Aries/Capricorn Risings are Astrology's hard-asses. You have a reputation for being a demanding teacher and a tough critic. You justify your behavior by saying you're no harder on others than you are on yourself, but the thing you have to watch out for here is that both Aries and Capricorn don't know when to quit. This is great when racing for the finish line or pushing a limit, not so great when you're dealing with others' shortcomings and insecurities. Aries isn't a big fan of weakness, and Capricorn never wants to make things easy.

You feel like you have a lot to prove. It comes from being born around midnight when the Sun is at the bottom of your horoscope. This creates the never-ending feeling that you will always be at the bottom of the barrel looking up. And it doesn't matter if you're at the top of the game, graduated first in your class, or routinely leave your competitors in the dust. This feeling will never go away—which is why it's up to you to temper it.

Do you know your own strength? It's often asked of people when they don't realize that they're more powerful than they think. You need to understand how powerful you truly are. You need to understand that you can do harm without meaning to. Aries/Capricorn Risings often wonder if they'll ever get to where they want to go in life—without recognizing that they arrived a long time ago.

# TAURUS SUN/CAPRICORN RISING

Success comes easy for you. That's because you're talented and blessed with a strong work ethic. You're one of the few people on the planet who knows what they're good at—and the fact that it was recognizable at a young age ensured that you got all the support, encouragement, and training you needed in order to thrive. The result is that there's no question that you'll accomplish what you set out to do in life. Now that doesn't mean you won't have to contend with day-to-day problems or will never come up against a wall or reach a dead end, but you know that things will work out eventually given time, effort, and ingenuity. It's important to identify what you do well and build on it—otherwise you waste your energy trying to be something you're not.

Taurus and Capricorn are both earth signs, which means that you need to have something to show for yourself at the end of the day. It can be a written page, a done deal, or money in your Venmo account; but whatever it is, it needs to be tangible. No personal revelation, spiritual insight, or cathartic experience for you. Your results have to be solid. That said, you don't have a lot of patience for people who blame circumstances for robbing them of their true calling or who long for the day when they will finally be free to do what they were always meant to do. You're a Taurus/Capricorn Rising. You know that time is short and that you have to make the most of it while you can. You don't dither or dabble or give up and go back the way you came. You power through because it's only by going the distance that you build the determination and endurance to get things done.

It's important to remember that even though you never had it easy—

and still don't—that's not the way people see you. They see you as success-ful. That's why it always rings false whenever you try to preach the gospel of work. Take the time to show them how to turn their circumstances around and the means by which they can enable themselves to do the things that they want to do. It's the greatest gift that you can give them.

# GEMINI SUN/CAPRICORN RISING

You had to learn the hard way to dumb it down. Raising your hand every time the teacher asked a question, solving the math problem that stymied classmates, and innocently volunteering guidance on how others could im-prove their performance didn't win you any friends. Instead of rising in their estimation you became the object of ridicule—or worse. It's likely you were called all sorts of names and had to suffer the indignity that goes along with it. Childhood isn't easy for Capricorn Risings. You can't help standing out as being more mature than your peers, which means paying a price for it. That's why you learned to agree when you clearly disagreed, to praise people who didn't deserve it, and to act like you didn't know some-thing when you did. It was in order to get along.

Living a double life is nothing new for a Gemini. It's kind of built into your sign. But like people who are closeted, pass as white, or don't identify with the body they were born into, that stress can build over time. And it's not just living an inauthentic life that's the problem. It's peopling your life with intimates and friends who have no idea of who you are, people whom you have to pretend with at work or at play or in the bedroom.

What begins as survival—editing out parts of yourself in order to get along—can eventually imperil your survival if you don't make adjustments. Survival mechanisms are like clothes—you outgrow them over time. The choices you had to make when you were a kid don't always translate to adulthood, and talents that once came so easily won't be as accessible after years of neglect.

There comes a time in a Gemini/Capricorn Rising's life when you have to reclaim that part of your horoscope that got suppressed. It's not unlike the reunification of Germany following the collapse of the Berlin Wall. It seems rather straightforward—just reunite two sides of yourself that should never have been separated—but it will prove to be a lot more difficult in the doing. Nevertheless, you will prevail. Few horoscopes are as resourceful and inventive as a Capricorn/Gemini Rising. What you get in the end is a fully realized life instead of one that's divided against itself.

## CANCER SUN/CAPRICORN RISING

Why do you always deny yourself the things you want most? As soon as someone shows interest or an appealing situation that's got your name on it becomes available—you retreat. It's amazing the reasons you'll come up with to keep your heart's desire at arm's length. One might think you don't want things to work out given all the complications you introduce, but no: It's actually built into your horoscope. The shortest distance between two points is a circle when you're a Cancer/Capricorn Rising. Nothing is ever straightforward; the path is always circuitous, which means you often have to lose something first in order to recognize what you had and it's only by journeying to get it back that you discover how much you treasured it all along.

One might say that this is your way of testing. Capricorn Risings often poke and prod at things to see if there's a trap lying underneath, but actually you're pretty clueless when it comes to your own feelings. When you're born at Sunset like you are then it's much easier for you to nurture everyone else than it is to nurture yourself. Your focus is on other people and you will protect their interests, safeguard their well-being, and stand by them through thick and thin. Yet when it comes to your own wants and needs you're at a complete loss. Paramours are greeted with blank expressions when they express what they feel about you or they're treated to long rambling monologues that clearly communicate your discomfort with things getting serious. It's ironic how you can be so comforting and reassuring with a total stranger but tongue-tied around someone who wants to get close. If you could squirt a cloud of ink and then make your escape—you would.

A Rising Sign that naturally distances itself paired with a Sun that's as far away from the Ascendant as possible shows that you have an intimacy problem. And since people aren't mind readers it's up to you to communicate what's going on inside. That takes time. And usually it's more time than most people have, but for those select few who are willing to wait— you won't disappoint. Once you've decided that you really do want someone, you will move heaven and earth to be by their side.

# LEO SUN/CAPRICORN RISING

You're everyone's favorite dad—even if you're a woman. They see you as a protector, a provider, and someone willing to shoulder the heavy burdens that others are looking to unload. Yet you don't do this to absolve anyone of their obligations, but rather to show them how it's done. You believe in biting the bullet. You also believe that people are a lot more capable than they think, which is why you won't race to their rescue. You'll let them flounder first. Often criticized for being too hands-off in a moment of crisis, you know that given enough space people will figure out the solution to their problems themselves. And when they do, they'll thank you for it. You're OK with playing the "bad guy" if the end result is someone learning to stand on their own two feet. After all, putting up with temper tantrums and smiling through the insults are what dads do.

You're genuinely bewildered and even hurt when you're told that you're too strict and demanding. Yes, you can be hard to please, but that's not because you're unbending. Leos are by their nature aspirational. Like the Sun, you will rise to the highest point in the sky to be the best that you can be. This resonates with your Capricorn Rising, which instinctively climbs every mountain it sees. Excellence is something you strive for and you're not going to achieve it if the bar is lowered. That's why you won't celebrate someone for being less than they can be. You'd only be letting them down.

Leo/Capricorn Risings feel a personal responsibility to set an example. You would never ask of anyone else something that you wouldn't ask of yourself. This is why you often find yourself making the sacrifices and taking the hits that you do. Loved ones and friends can't keep track of all the times when you've stood on principle, resisted conforming, or made the valiant effort only to be punished for it in the end. You've been chewed out plenty of times for taking the high road when a quick skip down the low one would do. But your answer is you wouldn't be able to live with yourself. Thankfully the Stars smile on this kind of bravery, as do the many people who follow in your footsteps.

# VIRGO SUN/CAPRICORN RISING

You're proud of your accomplishments. Everything you did, you did on your own. This bestows a confidence that nobody can take away or undermine. You didn't strategize or schmooze to get to where you are today. You skipped the shortcuts, declined the helping hands, and passed on the free passes. You came up from the bottom in true rags-to-riches fashion, which means that you own who you are. But there's more to your success than just ambition and discipline. It's the way you think. You carefully size up every foothold before you take it, like a climber free soloing up the face of a cliff. You leave nothing to chance, yet live in the moment. And that's why you're so evasive when people ask you what your secret is. How can you tell them that you never had a game plan and that you're still making things up as you go along?

For two zodiac signs famously identified with micromanagement and repression, it's ironic how spontaneous Virgo/Capricorn Risings can be. Virgos are known for spending more time with the footnotes than the book they're reading, and Capricorns are so calculated that they're in danger of snuffing the life out of any creative venture—but somehow, together, these two signs work through their apprehension and fear to produce something magnificent. Maybe it's your commitment to mastering the steps that frees you to dance right through them or constant repetition that results in a virtuosic fluency. In any case yours is one of the most daring and creative of zodiac sign combinations—although you would never say that out loud.

Your expertise speaks for itself. It shows in your craftsmanship and your attention to detail. Your decision to find the one thing that you're good at and then excel at it pays off. And it doesn't matter if it's bookkeeping or being a concert pianist—you will pursue it with a single-minded focus that people often confuse with passion. But it's not passion. There's nothing heated or embattled about what you do. The more likely word is— *devotion*. Only devotion can describe how you never grow tired or bored, how you approach a new project with all the freshness of when you started out. That same devotion also applies to your relationship. Like swans, you mate for life.

# LIBRA SUN/CAPRICORN RISING

Anyone who thinks they're getting an answer right away has another think coming. Your careful weighing of pros and cons combined with a distilled assessment for what the future consequences might be means that you're in no hurry to deliver your verdict. And it doesn't matter how much people pressure you to make up your mind. You will not be swayed. You bring as much seriousness to your lunch order as you do to your portfolio investments. Loved ones and friends know better than to surprise you with any last-minute requests because you simply won't respond. You're like the

Supreme Court. They don't take a look at anything unless it's gone through the proper channels—and like the Supreme Court, whatever decision you make is final.

Countless lovers have been left cooling their heels—not to mention sellers waiting to hear back from you and companies obediently revising a contract yet again. Clearly there have been many missed opportunities—not everyone's going to be so patient—but you don't care. Anything that feels hurried or harried isn't worth it as far as you're concerned. You do things in your own time and only fraternize with people who understand that.

Everything you do is done with an eye on the bigger picture. The Sun at the top of your chart means that you can literally see for miles and miles from your vantage point. You may be tempted by things in the here and now—like a pleasant diversion or an easy out—but ultimately you will put it aside in favor of what matters most. At times this can strike people as self-denial bordering on masochism. Little do they realize that everything is carefully calculated as to how much more you'll gain in the end.

Venus, ruler of Libra, gives you the appeal of a highly coveted prize. Add Capricorn Rising and that prize is sure to be placed on a shelf out of reach. This is why so many people treat you as something rarified and unattainable. You could get seduced into thinking of yourself this way as well if you allow it to happen. But if you don't want to wind up locked away in some ivory tower then you need to learn to let your hair down. Not to just anyone, surely, but you do need to let it down.

# SCORPIO SUN/CAPRICORN RISING

You want to be on top. This isn't the same thing as being outstanding in your field or winning every contest you enter. You're not into status or accolades. It's about being in control. You're acutely aware of what happens when you give away your power. You've suffered at the hands of lovers who didn't appreciate you, bosses who didn't recognize you, and parents who didn't know what to do with you. You've spent years trying to fit into other people's expectations only to learn that they were far lower than the ones you held for yourself. Even your fear of rejection was fueled more by your dread than anything that actually devastated you. That's because you are tougher than most and can take a lot of punishment. Once you realize that you're the one holding yourself back then everything changes. Lovers accommodate you, bosses pass over the reins, and clients do what they're told. It's remarkable how easy it is to get your way once your perspective shifts.

Scorpio/Capricorn Risings are often described as scary ambitious. Part Machiavelli, part Gordon Gekko, the general consensus is you won't settle for anything less than complete world domination. You're power-mad. Needless to say Scorpio/Capricorn Risings are far too realistic in their aims and ethical in their approaches. You want to succeed at attaining your goal, not overreach your grasp. Nor are you the heartless creatures that other zodiac signs make you out to be. Scorpio/Capricorn Risings are deeply feeling and just as reluctant to show it. You're the ones most likely to do a good turn for someone who bad-mouthed you because you understand that it came from a place of pain. Of course, it's done out of sight and without ever calling attention to it.

*Curmudgeonly* is a word often used with you. Mars is irascible by nature and Saturn has never been known to suffer fools gladly. Some Scorpio/ Capricorn Risings will try to hide all of this behind an agreeable veneer, but it's never truly convincing. It always comes across as forced. Nevertheless, you have a wicked wit to go along with that deadpan delivery so you're quick to recover from any social blunders. If anything, people who felt hurt are the first ones to laugh because it makes them look smart.

# SAGITTARIUS SUN/CAPRICORN RISING

You keep on going long after everyone else has called it quits. Not only do you have the courage of your convictions, but your convictions are deepened by the dilemmas you face. Now this isn't to say that you'll stand by what you believe in. There have been plenty of times when you've abandoned a cause or refused to speak up when it mattered most, and these failures never sit well with you. You were born with a constant conscience that doesn't let you off the hook. It will always bring you back to that crossroads where you turned left instead of right until you remedy the situation.

You learn as much from your faults as you do from your merits. Maybe even more so since you're a Sagittarius/Capricorn Rising. Neither zodiac sign wants to be in the wrong. Sagittarius can have an inexhaustible zealotry—outshouting anyone who tries to contradict it—while Capricorn is so poised and polished in its presentation that everyone just assumes that you know what you're talking about. This could turn into a dangerous combination if you didn't insist on being accountable. It can be agonizing at times—especially when it would be easier not to say anything—but you will always take responsibility for the things you've done, even if that results in shame and ostracism.

Your path in life may be random and meandering. Full of setbacks and confounding tangents, it often looks as if you're deliberately trying to get lost; however, if you were to look back over your shoulder at where you've been you would recognize a running through line. Many people choose a career or a calling and stick to it. They never deviate from their course. You, on the other hand, keep coming back to yours—no matter the missteps and misjudgments—and every time you do you discover something new and inspirational. Typical Capricorn Risings have their eyes set on the bar that's always being raised higher. Your bent is more spiritual. You're focused on the meaning of things rather than the payoff. If there's a lesson to be learned from all that you've endured then that lesson makes the experience worth it. Your accomplishments may not look like much on the outside but that doesn't stop people from seeking out your wisdom and guidance.

# AQUARIUS RISING

People can sense that you're different. There's something about you that's wise beyond your years, more sophisticated than your background, and accelerated in development. It's a peculiar

**People can sense that you're different.**

quality that says: "I am not from around here." And it doesn't matter if your entire family was present at your delivery, they still can't help wondering if you were switched at birth or the product of alien DNA. You will always come across as "one of these things that's not like the others." It's an ironic fate for a Rising Sign that longs to fit in.

Words like *eccentric*, *quirky*, and *weird* are often used to describe an Aquarius Rising. There's this general assumption that you deliberately choose to be odd and rebellious and that you're doing it for the attention. Nothing could be further from the truth. Childhood can be a particularly cruel time as kids have little kindness for others who don't conform. Some Aquarius Risings respond by becoming even more flamboyant, out there, or geeky, while others will consciously edit out parts of their behavior that they feel are socially unacceptable. But even if you do succeed in making yourself more presentable—dressing like everyone else or dumbing down your speech—it still won't convince anyone that you belong. Aquarius is a fiercely contrarian sign.

Aquarius is ruled by two planets—Saturn and Uranus. Saturn is as conventional as Uranus is unconventional, which means that nothing sits right with you because you have to honor both energies. There are as many Aquarius Risings living happily straitlaced button-down lives as there are Aquarius Risings who never stop plotting to overthrow the establishment. But look a little closer and you'll see the straitlaced types introducing progressive reforms into traditionally corporate structures while the revolutionaries plant the seeds of grassroots organizations that grow into well-funded and respectable institutions.

The biggest problem with an Aquarius Ascendant is that you're perceived as cold and aloof. It comes from having a winter sign as your horoscopic face. And it doesn't matter how effervescent and friendly you are, people just assume you don't have feelings—or at least the kind that can be hurt. They also don't think that you want to be touched or held close, which is why they keep a polite distance. If you want more intimacy in your life then it's up to you to do something about it. It's awkward because you can't help feeling selfish simply for asking to hold hands, but nobody's going to approach you otherwise. You do such a great job of appearing to be above it all that everyone assumes you like it up there.

## AQUARIUS SUN/AQUARIUS RISING

Everyone notices your eyes right away. Dazzling and otherworldly, one can't help but admire their electric beauty. You have this piercing gaze that sees right through people. It almost feels like being examined with X-ray vision. This is great if you're out on a date with someone who wants to get naked, but it can prove unsettling for co-workers who feel like you're reading their minds or bosses nervous about maintaining their superior rank. Most people are told to lower their voice. When you're an Aquarius with Aquarius Rising you're often asked to tone down the stare.

Everything with you is transparent. It has to be when you're your own zodiac sign rising. There's no deflecting attention or muddying the waters. And nothing's more important to an Aquarius/Aquarius Rising than the truth. But it's not a personal truth based on what only you think or a creed born of spiritual faith. What you're after is an indisputable truth that transcends opinions, feelings, and privilege. You want everything to be out in the open for the whole world to see. That's why you freely disclose information that would make a reality star blush, welcome criticisms others would dodge, and suggest an even tougher line of questioning than the one already being posed in an interview. Others wonder if you don't derive a self-righteous satisfaction in all of this, but no. Your thinking is quite simple. How can you ask for total accountability from anyone else if you don't demonstrate it yourself?

Aquarians tend to come from a wild and crazy background. You doubly so. People aren't so much astonished by the stories you have to share as they are by the twists and turns and unexpected revelations. And perhaps it's the revelations that are the most surprising. You will coolly narrate some pretty harrowing episodes of loss and betrayal as if they had all happened to someone else—never once exhibiting any pain or sadness. Like an accident victim ready to walk away from the wreckage, one can't help but wonder if you're still in shock.

You may not recognize your emotional scars, but others do. It's why lovers and friends are always talking to you about your feelings. It's the one truth you have problems seeing—even if it is as plain as the nose on your face.

# PISCES SUN/AQUARIUS RISING

People wonder what you're thinking. You have such a profound and faraway look on your face. It's why they're always asking if things are OK. There's something about you that's hard to fathom.

It warms your heart to think that anyone notices. You often assume they don't. When you're a Pisces Sun with Aquarius Rising you feel like the invisible man. Not an absent one—you're definitely a presence that leaves behind smudges and footprints—but an unremarkable one that others walk past. This comes from the fact that Pisces and Aquarius are selfless by nature. Pisces draws from a bottomless well of empathy while Aquarius never thinks it's done anything special to warrant the attention.

Yet you were born with a poet's soul and a scientist's mind. Your Pisces Sun gives you your love of symbols, which is why you're fluent in music and math. Your affinity for notes, glyphs, and numbers allows you to arrange and rearrange them in countless variations. You'd make a killer coder or a jazz musician. Typically, a Pisces Sun is only too happy daydreaming about all the possibilities; it's the Aquarius Rising that pushes you to organize your thoughts and actually sketch something out. There's an unmistakable genius to this zodiacal combination, but the question is: Do you even recognize it?

Money is an issue when you're born just before Sunrise. You may have been raised in a household where your parents struggled to make ends meet. This could have led you to lower your sights; to choose security over aspiration. The good thing about having an Aquarius Rising is things denied to you early on come full circle later in life. Pisces/Aquarius Risings often go back to school to get their degree or develop their talent after years of toil. But there's still this reluctance to show off what you can *really* do.

We have the Pisces/Aquarius Risings to thank for being the unspoken angels in our lives. You're the ones who turn around the lost causes, slip food into hungry hands, or make anonymous donations to favorite charities culled from the savings tucked under your mattress. People always wonder why you don't do more for yourself. They don't understand the bigger picture: that doing for others *is* doing for yourself because it makes the world a better place.

# ARIES SUN/AQUARIUS RISING

You're Astrology's MVP. You may not be the star athlete leading the team to victory, but everyone knows that victory couldn't happen without you. You're the shortstop who picks off the player who's strayed off base, the corps dancer who can jump into any role last minute, or the spelling-bee champ that teammates can count on to power through in the eleventh hour. The general public may never know who you are, but you're legendary to people in the industry.

You like playing a supporting role. People in leadership positions may get all the glory, but there's no denying the aggravation that comes along with it. You don't envy them the burden of responsibility or the pressure to perform. By locating that sweet spot between top dog and the rest of the pack you're free to do what you do best without the glad-handing, ass-kissing, and campaigning that goes into being number one.

But you wouldn't be an Aries if you didn't have a competitive streak. Ruled by the planet Mars, you're always on the lookout for a worthy opponent—someone who's gunning for you and whose prowess challenges you to up your game. Aries Sun/Aquarius Risings baffle their contemporaries because they're always making friends with the enemy. People try to tell you to stick to your side of the fence but you refuse to do it. Why? Because you like hanging out in their company. There's a mutual respect that comes from understanding what it's like to be in the other one's shoes. You know that an opponent will tell you things your friends won't. Friends tell you what you want to hear because they're protective; an opponent will tell you the things you need to hear because they're not invested in your feelings. They know a lot about you because they've studied you.

Aquarius is always learning from people. Astrologers say it's because Aquarius is the humanitarian sign, but that's not true. Sagittarius and Pisces are far more generous and forgiving. What Aquarius does is never allow for prejudice to get in the way. You can't learn if you've decided you're smarter than everyone else. All you do is set yourself up for failure and when you're an Aries Sun/Aquarius Rising the last thing you ever want to do is lose your competitive edge.

# TAURUS SUN/AQUARIUS RISING

You're here to set people up in life. Maybe you're the Realtor who sells them their first home, the banker who approves their business loan, or the commercial property owner who leases out space. Taurus is the most territorial sign of the zodiac and your Sun's placement at the base of your astrological chart speaks to your need for roots, home, and security. These are the things that create a sense of permanence in a world where things often fall apart unexpectedly. Nobody succeeds without a strong foundation, which is why you're in the business of helping people to establish themselves.

At first glance this appears to contradict your Rising Sign's reputation for storming the barricades. Isn't Aquarius supposed to be a wild-eyed radical, the sworn enemy of the moneyed elite? Perhaps. But deep down you're a Taurus, not an Aquarius, which means you need to see something solid for your efforts. Let others engage in ideological clashes if that's their thing, your focus is on transforming the landscape. Taurus is the zodiac sign of the gardener, and like a gardener you work from the ground up. You don't try to impose, override, or force a fit. Everything you do is organic and if it takes a while to produce results then so be it. You're in no rush. Taurus Sun/ Aquarius Risings are the quiet revolutionaries.

Taurus Sun/Aquarius Risings show up a lot in urban planning. They're also fond of architectural design and curating art exhibits. Aquarius is conceptual and Taurus likes to get its hands dirty. But physical space isn't the only kind of space that needs zoning; there are safe spaces as well. Staunchly protective signs, Taurus guards the sanctuary while Aquarius is an unflinching defender of human rights.

Taurus has a reputation for being materialistic, but it's still a Venus-ruled sign, which means it likes to make people happy. And what makes people happy more than pleasures and delights? Sustainability. You're probably the relative who gives savings bonds instead of computer games, but that's because you can't help but take in the bigger picture when you're a Taurus/Aquarius Rising. You know full well that if you give people what they want they'll just consume it and come back hungry for more. But educate them about cultivating their resources and they will learn to make their garden grow.

# GEMINI SUN/AQUARIUS RISING

You don't stand out in a crowd. And that's not because you're unremarkable in appearance or easily overlooked. You're actually quite stylish if not a touch avant-garde. No, the reason you don't stand out in a crowd is because you don't stand still. When one asks after you at a party, for instance, chances are everyone's seen you but they don't know where you are exactly. They'll say you were just here, that they last saw you over there, or probably you just left. You often get worried texts from lost friends who don't realize that they're standing right next to you.

A strange mix of irreverent and respectable, Gemini/Aquarius Risings are contrarian by nature. You'll take up the opposite side of an argument without a second thought for whether it's right or not. You're seized by the impulse to speak for the side that isn't being spoken for. One would think this stems from a moral obligation to defend those who can't defend themselves, but your investment isn't personal. You'd immediately switch sides if the occasion arose. This strikes people who don't know you as thoughtless and disloyal. They don't understand how you could be for something one moment and then against it the next. What they're missing is your Aquarian Ascendant's commitment to the truth. The truth isn't something set in stone. It has to be sought after, questioned, and challenged. Truth isn't supposed to be *the* answer but rather an "aha" moment that appears briefly in the scuffle of rigorous debate.

Now not every Gemini/Aquarius Rising is going to become a lawyer, scientist, or political activist. It can get too long-winded and exhausting. However, you will gravitate toward positions that utilize that marvelous mind of yours. There are people who are born with active imaginations. You were born with an active intellect and it needs developing and finetuning. Otherwise you become anxious and irritable.

Think about adopting some kind of physical regimen like running or swimming. Air signs have a tendency to disregard their bodies. You really do subscribe to the maxim "mind over matter." This can help you to power through obstacles in the moment but it takes a toll in the long run. Building a strong relationship to your body helps you inhabit it more comfortably and see it as something more than just a necessary evil.

## CANCER SUN/AQUARIUS RISING

Cancer is the family-first sign of the zodiac. Blood is thicker than water as shown by the way you will unhesitatingly put your child's, parent's, or sibling's needs above those of a boss or even a lover. And it doesn't matter if you were raised in a dysfunctional home. You will drop everything to go look after your tribe. You don't miss a birthday and assiduously plan your schedule around holiday get-togethers. Anyone you date has to pass muster with your clan. That includes Aunt Bea. And should you decide to marry then they need to be from the same background. Some Cancer Suns have been known to marry outside their faith but only after their intended spouse has converted or agreed to raise their offspring according to tradition.

To be born with Aquarius Rising means that you can't shut the door on anyone. This isn't a moral mandate as much as it is a horoscopic one. You will find yourself in situations where you have to be there for people who aren't like you. This is good because it gets you to expand your world. Maybe you befriend the kid who gets picked on by everyone else, become roommates with someone from a foreign country, or work side by side with people you never would have fraternized with otherwise. Not only does this encourage you to question your assumptions, but it also gets you to recognize your prejudices and ultimately to discard them. It's hard to harden your heart toward people you hang with.

It's the Aquarius Rising that gives the impression you're just a naïve do-gooder. It's the part of you that can't help reading up on all the right ways to be and then telling people how to live. Aquarius can be a bit parochial in its delivery—especially when it feels uncomfortable. This is why you're better off going with what comes naturally rather than what you think you should do. Don't second-guess those Cancer Sun instincts. They will never lead you astray.

Cancer/Aquarius Risings often find themselves living in households very different from the one they imagined yet rooted in the best that family can bring. Family isn't the one you were born into; it's the one you make and when you're a Cancer/Aquarius Rising there's room at the table for everybody.

# LEO SUN/AQUARIUS RISING

You've always been the odd one. Maybe you were the brain, had the funny name, or matured too early so you couldn't cover up the fact that you were physically further along than the rest of the kids. Any of these would have made you the object of derision, but that never really happened. That's because you projected a fixity of purpose. You still do to this day. On other horoscopes this might appear prideful or superior, but on yours it just comes across as someone with a place to go. And like with most people intent on reaching their destination, you never waver from your course.

Success is something every Leo experiences once in their lifetime. When you're a Leo/Aquarius Rising you will experience success a number of times—and each in a new and definitive way. To others it may appear as if you've had a plan all along, but to you these successes are an abiding mystery, unpredictable occurrences that happen only at the right time and place. Now that's not to say that you don't work hard to achieve them, because you do. But they're so random and their circumstances so unlikely that you can't help but feel like you're on some cosmic scavenger hunt with each success pointing the way to the next.

The father plays a powerful role in every Leo's life, but because you were born when the Sun was setting it's likely that yours wasn't around. This creates a longing for approval that doesn't really square with your Aquarius Rising. If anything, your Rising Sign steers you away from anything conventional or sentimental. Yet that need is still there, which might explain your strange devotion to father figures who don't deserve it—or worse, exploit you. Ultimately you walk away from them—Aquarius is an irrepressible rebel and has to do things its own way—but it's not without your having learned something valuable from them in the process. You may dismiss them in public, but you still cling to them in private.

Your relationship is very important to you. It may take forever to find the right person, but when you do, you mate for life. This isn't to say that you don't have your dalliances—your Aquarian Ascendant makes you a people person—but the marriage always comes first.

# VIRGO SUN/AQUARIUS RISING

You refuse to be labeled. You understand that this is most people's automatic shorthand, a way of remembering who you are for their future reference, but you're also sensitive to the assumptions and associations that go along with being categorized. Once you agree to a label, you're signing on to its history and giving up yours. It's why you won't hesitate to point out that labels are often artificial constructs aimed at reinforcing institutionalized biases. This can sometimes create awkward moments when you're being introduced casually or at work, but you'll suffer through them. As far as you're concerned it's no different than correcting someone who's confused you with somebody else or keeps mispronouncing your name. You don't see it as being rude. You see it as helping out.

This impulse to educate is reflected in your Sun Sign's commitment to accuracy and your Rising Sign's mission to enlighten wherever it can. It comes from a sincere place. Unfortunately, it can also create the impression of being a know-it-all. Most people don't take kindly to corrections—

especially when they feel like they're being called out. It's only natural for them to become defensive or even retaliatory. This is why it's so important for you to exercise the communication skills that are at your disposal.

One of Virgo's great disarming qualities is humility. You have no problem sharing the most mortifying moments of your life and you won't think twice about narrating them in hilarious detail. But you do more than just *own* your mistakes—you learn from them. And it's by demonstrating how you became a better person as a result that you can help others to do the same. Self-improvement is your crusade. It's why you like to show off your before-and-after pictures.

The thing you have to work on is patience and respect for others' processes. Virgo/Aquarius Risings tend to get militant in their approach. You believe that if you can get people to follow certain specified steps then they will arrive at the desired outcome. But not everyone is built the same way— which is a peculiar blind spot for a Sun Sign/Rising Sign combination that celebrates diversity as much as you do. Only by stepping away from the theorizing and focusing on one-on-one mentoring instead will you achieve results that are as individual as they are singular.

# LIBRA SUN/AQUARIUS RISING

You make a peculiar first impression. Maybe it's your formal manner, the hard-to-identify accent, or the way you talk as if there was a third party listening in. Sometimes you have such a distant and searching expression that the person you're talking to can't help but turn around to see if you're looking at someone else. You don't mean to come across as poised and statuesque, but it can't be helped. It's what comes from being constantly scrutinized.

You can literally see yourself as an object in space—almost as if you were hovering outside your body like an astral projection. All Aquarius Risings have this ability to switch into remote-viewing mode, to observe yourself as if you were watching your interactions on a security camera. That's why you're your best critic when it comes to reviewing your own job performance. You know what was on, what was off, and what can be improved upon for next time. You're so on top of things that even critics have a hard time finding something to pick apart.

Libra/Aquarius Risings are so polished in their appearance that people just naturally stand taller or suck in their gut tighter when you walk into a room. They want to be classy just like you. Yet for all of your refinement and sophistication, you've never lost your common touch. You could be dressed to the nines with a flat tire out in the middle of nowhere and you'd be all right. Not only would someone be along in no time, but they would happily help you out of your jam and send you on your way. You love people and people love you. That's why you're never worried about walking alone late at night or attending a social event where you don't know a soul.

Ironically, being a friend to everyone leaves you vulnerable to what others think. The Sun is weakest in Libra, which means it's hard for you to go against prevailing opinion. Thankfully your Aquarius Rising is enough of a renegade that any relationship that was frowned upon at first is eventually salvaged, but it takes a while for that to happen—leaving you in the awkward position of having to apologize to a romantic partner for how long it took to see the light.

# SCORPIO SUN/AQUARIUS RISING

You have a pretty good idea of what people are capable of and it's not pretty. This may stem from your own personal upbringing or the injustices you've witnessed in life. A lot of things have happened to you that no one should have to endure, yet you took it all on the chin. In fact, to hear you tell it, nothing seems to faze you. Where others may cover their eyes or bury their faces into their lover's shoulder during the gory part of a horror movie, you will sit there and make yourself watch. When you're a Scorpio Sun with Aquarius Rising you never look away.

Someone has to tell the story and that person is you. But nobody's going to believe it if you're too emotionally involved or fail to get the facts straight. It's why you work assiduously to present a dispassionate report. You deliberately strip it of any speculation and let the information speak for itself. Most people have to train themselves to be this precise and exacting but you come by it naturally. Perhaps too naturally.

Scorpio/Aquarius Risings are a unique mix of cynicism and idealism. Your Scorpio Sun knows better than to take anything at face value. Everyone has a hidden agenda, a reason for disguising what they want most in the world. Maybe it's built around greed, pain, or self-preservation, but that ulterior motive is there. The question isn't so much whether you can trust someone as much as it's: Do your needs dovetail? This is the variable constantly being factored into your calculus.

Your Aquarius Ascendant, on the other hand, refuses to accept that everyone's a bottom-feeder. Aquarius can be just as fixed on its quest to realize the best in humanity as Scorpio is on exposing the worst, and although your

Rising Sign must ultimately genuflect to the Sun—you were born with your Sun at the highest point in your horoscope—it will still try to turn your gaze up. This is why you can never harden your heart no matter how justified the reasons and why revenge never tastes as sweet as you initially imagined.

Scorpio/Aquarius Risings often come across as cold and indifferent, but like a slumbering volcano that passes as a gentle mountain, that impression is only skin-deep. You will always think—and feel—too much.

# SAGITTARIUS SUN/AQUARIUS RISING

It must be delightful to never lose that sense of wonder as you scroll through pictures of exotic countries that couldn't be more different from the one you live in, learn about newly discovered species that were tucked inside the pockets of creation all along, or gaze up at stars that are not at all like the ones that people wish upon half a world away. You are at home in all this bigness, which is why you're still asking those searching questions that college kids ponder at four thirty in the morning long after the party has wound down. Your world never gets small even if some of the people around you do.

You're used to talking until all hours of the night. It began with that foreign exchange student you dated and continues today with clients scattered across different time zones. People assume you're a night owl because of the time stamps on your emails, but actually you're not. When you're a Sagittarius Sun with Aquarius Rising you are perpetually wired. You never know when your eyes are going to fly open and your mind will start downloading all the latest pressing concerns. You know exactly what twenty-four hours in a day feels like because you've hung out in every one of them.

You'd make a great pilot or flight attendant. Getting out to see the world is every Sagittarian's dream. But it's just as likely that you work in the financial markets, a global company, a hospital, or anywhere else that's never heard of nine to five. This constant changing of the hours suits you. You were born with your own unique circadian rhythm. Moreover, your Rising Sign's ability to disconnect from the body makes you almost impervious to jet lag or even sleep deprivation.

It takes you a long time to settle down. Sagittarius/Aquarius Risings are famously restless and are usually the non-marrying type. This has less to do with safeguarding your freedom and more to do with whether a partner can keep up with you. You don't want your horizons narrowed because someone lost their spirit of adventure. You often form lasting relationships with people from faraway places—you do your best sleeping on airplanes— and if you were to have children then you'd want at least one from every continent. Including Antarctica.

## CAPRICORN SUN/AQUARIUS RISING

You just want to be left alone, but that's not going to happen. It doesn't matter if you're hiding out in a library, retreating to a monastery, or living in the backwoods—people will still seek you out. And this isn't because of some reputed scandal or secret past. You emit a wisdom and knowledge that others want to be around. It's why they will follow you no matter how hard you try to elude them. It's a problem that haunted the desert fathers back in Egypt so you're in good company.

Capricorn is a solitary sign. It comes from being born under Saturn, a planet famous for keeping its distance. Now this isn't to say that you're misanthropic or an agoraphobe. You enjoy people. But you also treasure your time away from them when you can be alone with your work and your books. Studious and contemplative, you delight in the depth of thinking that only silence brings.

However, your Ascendant has other plans in store for you. Like a concerned parent worried that you're becoming antisocial, your Aquarius Rising is always ushering people into your life. It's constantly putting you in contact with lost souls, emotional basket cases, or penitent sinners looking for redemption. But these aren't just losers who are down on their luck. They're diamonds in the rough in need of your attention. As a Capricorn Sun with Aquarius Rising it's up to you to bring out their better angels.

Your influence is greater than you think and you need to consider that. Some people are loud with nothing to say while others are charismatic with little to show for themselves. They take up a lot of space. Your influence is like a voice in the night. You have a way of speaking that makes people feel like you're talking directly to them. Evocative and soothing, your vocal tone resonates on a soul level. You may not believe that you have this effect, but you do. Capricorn/Aquarius Risings make great chanteuses or late-night radio hosts.

The thing you have to watch out for is self-abnegation. The desert fathers were fond of donning hair shirts, flogging themselves, or going for long periods without food or water. It's doubtful that you would be this extreme, but the tendency is still there. You can never practice enough self-love.

# PISCES RISING

People see what they want to see in you. Like the ocean which changes color according to the sky overhead, you reflect what they project. Now this isn't to say that you operate like a mirror or a blank screen. You're not some vacant expression waiting for someone to come along and lock eyes with you. Rather you have this way of stirring feelings in others without really doing anything. That's why strangers always ask if you've met before or swear that you look just like an ex-lover or childhood friend. Water rules memories and dreams so people don't think twice about telling you the most intimate things about themselves. Add Neptune, the ruler of Pisces, to the mix, and there's a fantasy element involved that can be wild and fun, but also leaves you wondering if they're even interested in getting to know you at all.

Nobody wants to be the figment of someone else's imagination. And as a Pisces Rising you're constantly struggling against the undertow of others' fascination. They see things in you that you can only guess at. Sometimes it's nice—like when you're an artist's muse or the object of desire. There's no denying it's better to be adored than reviled, but mostly it's exhausting because of the way you have to walk on eggshells. One false move might break

> **People see what they want to see in you.**

the spell and then where would you be? It's tedious competing with a romanticized version of you.

Now you could issue disclaimers and play down your attributes and plus points, but that would be like abdicating the most precious quality of your horoscope. Would a movie star ever let someone else take charge of their name, image, or brand? When you're a Pisces Rising you have something other people want—it might be a mystique, profundity, or a magical way of being in the world. Whatever it is, it can't be bottled, which is why you need to be aware of the image you're projecting and the effect that it has. It's not a good idea to be unconscious of something that impacts others' subconscious so profoundly.

Pisces Risings often come across as not being entirely here. Languid sighs and faraway looks leave partners wondering if you really want to do the relationship thing or bosses questioning if you'd be happier working somewhere else. Truth to tell, you don't really know. When you're a Pisces Rising you can't help but long for the things you cannot have. And the fact that you would still be yearning for something different even after you succeeded at realizing your most cherished dreams is hard to explain—even to yourself.

# PISCES SUN/PISCES RISING

You have this problem with getting talked into doing things you'll regret. Pisces people are often accused of being gullible—you have such a powerful imagination that you'll believe just about anything—but what this really stems from is not wanting to let anyone down. You can see how much a desire, wish, or hope means to another person and so you'll do whatever you can to help them attain it. And if that means stepping aside, making a sacrifice, or biting your tongue when the time to speak up matters most then you will. It's astounding how many opportunities you've thrown away because it would have deprived somebody else of something they wanted. You thought you were doing the right thing in the moment only to realize that that opportunity was meant for you. That job had your name on it. That lover wanted you and nobody else. A creative project was your brainchild, which is why it dissolved in the hands of a colleague who didn't possess your artistic vision.

These would all add up to a series of bitter disappointments if it weren't for the fact that you're a Pisces/Pisces Rising. Pisces has a problem with making itself a priority. People think it comes from selflessness, but actually it's a result of feeling things so deeply and expansively that it takes you forever to figure out what you're really experiencing in your heart. It would be like asking the ocean which drop of water it likes best. Thankfully the Sun was rising when you were born, which pushes you to the front of the line. You're *supposed* to get the things that you want—and you will no matter how many times you shoot yourself in the foot.

Neptune isn't the only ruler of your Ascendant; Jupiter is too. And it's Jupiter, the planet of good fortune and higher purpose, that ensures everything will turn out for the best. You may have to wander around in the desert for a while or do penance for the mistakes you made, but you'll eventually clue into the fact that denying yourself the blessings that Fate has given you is as criminal as taking something that isn't yours. Failing to be what you were meant to be deprives you and others of your gifts, your talents, and your love.

# ARIES SUN/PISCES RISING

Why is it you're always being called in too late—long past the point when you could have salvaged the situation? It's clear nothing can be done, yet people still look at you with a hopeful expression that maybe you can pull off some kind of miracle. You know better than to try—you should just say that it's out of your hands—but you never do. And it doesn't matter how many times you fail to resuscitate or come up short, as an Aries/Pisces Rising you never met a lost cause you could say no to. They're simply irresistible.

Does this make you self-defeatist? Not really. This idea that you're fated to arrive after the ship has sailed isn't something you made up. It's actually hardwired into your horoscope. You were born under Aries—the first sign of the zodiac—whereas your Rising Sign—Pisces—is the last. What that means is that things have to end before you can begin because Aries follows Pisces in zodiacal order. In other words, it's only after someone's made a mess of things that you're brought in. Proof of this lies in a repeating life pattern of filling in for the absent parent, covering for an incompetent supervisor, or inheriting a situation nobody else wants to go near. One could say you're being set up for failure, but few zodiac signs rise to the challenge like an Aries. It's how you grow. These "exercises in futility" build muscles and resilience so that you emerge with a refined skill set for managing fiascos and containing fallout. You may not arrive in time to avert a crisis, but you'll certainly help people deal with the aftermath.

Ironically, your biggest struggle is in letting yourself do the things you want. It's hard to be in a relationship or work on your own projects when you're Astrology's first responder. You continually suffer from Cosmic Interruptus. Nevertheless, you must train yourself to create something that's yours or you'll forever be putting off the things that matter. If you wait for the right time to finally live your life then you'll never live it. The plus side to being called away from something you cherish is that you have something to return to when you're done putting out other people's fires.

# TAURUS SUN/PISCES RISING

You don't think of yourself as being especially creative. That's because it all comes so naturally. You possess a natural feel for what textures go together, how color and light might mix and blend, and where a piece of furniture should go in order to create a sense of flow and balance in a space. It's almost like you have a mystic touch for making things more beautiful. But your talents are hardly consigned to the decorative arts. You can apply this same sense of flow to science, mathematics, or the most unimaginative business plan. It's not the materials that matter; it's your vision. You can see things that others don't and once engaged you will deconstruct and rearrange it with the knowing confidence of a child genius playing with a Rubik's Cube. It's that simple.

One wouldn't know that you possessed these abilities if they didn't know you personally. You probably weren't very good at school, didn't trumpet your accomplishments, and may even have shied away from competition. Although Taurus is methodical by nature, there's nothing saying that you have to do things the way others want them done. If anything, you may wait until nobody's around to roll up your sleeves and get to work. You don't like anyone looking over your shoulder or cramping your style with their expectations. You prefer to go off and do your own thing and then come back with the finished product in hand.

Pisces Risings are reluctant to promote themselves so thankfully your workmanship speaks for itself. Your ability to spin straw into gold leaves others astonished and wanting more. However, your Pisces Rising is so humble and self-effacing that it gives people the impression that you're just doing it for the love of doing it. You are, but thank heavens your Taurus Sun knows that nothing's free in this world. Where other artistic types get stressed out talking money, your Taurus Sun will just say that your fee is non-negotiable. The plus side to having your Sun Sign and Rising Sign ruled by benefic influences—Venus rules Taurus and Jupiter rules Pisces—is that people will eventually come around to paying your asking price. You know that what you produce is top quality and that they won't be able to find anything like it anywhere else.

## GEMINI SUN/PISCES RISING

People often mistake you for something you're not. They think you're superficial when you're deep, conservative when you're liberal, and gay when you're straight. At first you felt like you had to correct them, but as you've grown older you've discovered that it's much more fun to see where the conversation goes. You never know what might come up. And though you're repeatedly accused of being misleading, you're extremely careful not to say anything that would confirm or deny. Labeling is other people's problem, not yours.

Your look is always changing. Part of this stems from your love of fashion, but in truth your appearance alters according to what piece of clothing you wear. Put on an oversized jersey and you look dope, try on a power suit and people would swear you were a member of the Fortune 500. You do more than rock the look. You become the look—which is why it's so easy for you to disappear into whatever character you're playing. Gemini/Pisces Risings are the preferred horoscope of actors, undercover agents, and con artists.

It's the evasive quality that others find a little . . . untrustworthy. Changing the subject, dodging questions, or rarely offering a clear-cut explanation creates the impression that you're not being entirely straightforward. And you aren't—but that's not necessarily because you've got something to hide. A Gemini will guard their options as stubbornly as a Sagittarius will defend their freedom. You have a visceral response to being pinned down to anything. Even if it's something you were planning on doing anyway, you will deliberately change your mind if you feel like you're playing into others' expectations. You may even lie about your feelings just so someone doesn't get the idea that they matter as much as they do.

Geminis are excellent wordsmiths. You know how to say the things people want to hear without actually saying it. Add to this your Pisces Rising's gift for nuance and insinuation and is it any wonder that no two people can agree on the conversation you just had? But be careful not to focus so much on the loopholes that you never commit to what you wanted in the first place. You don't want to let the things that really matter slip through your fingers like water.

# CANCER SUN/PISCES RISING

If you could adopt every orphaned child and rescue any neglected animal, you would. Your heart is so big and your compassion so limitless that the idea of anyone being left out in the cold keeps you up nights. It's a good thing you weren't in charge of Noah's Ark. You would never have stopped at two of each. You're the one who will drive a dog hundreds of miles to be united with its new forever friend, who sponsors trees being planted in countries you'll never visit, and refuses to give up on a loved one—even if this is their sixth stint in rehab. Cancers aren't usually so magnanimous. Safeguarding their family is their number one priority and, though famous for motherly love and devotion, Cancers have no problem raising the draw-bridge and filling the moat when it comes to the plight of people who "aren't like us." It's your Pisces Rising that leads you to administer to the disadvantaged, bundle up the lost, and in some cases break the law to provide sanctuary.

You're often in trouble with friends and neighbors who see you as constantly opening the door to anything that scratches at it. Not only do they regard you as a bleeding heart that can't be cauterized, they wonder if you aren't trying to antagonize them by deliberately espousing causes you know are unwelcome and fly in the face of the status quo. You have been on the wrong side of more arguments than you can count and yet you persist. And it's not like you're rebellious or have a point to prove. If anything, you're deeply devout. That's why it hurts when you're forced to choose sides or curb your charitable impulses.

People with Pisces Rising in their horoscope have historically been in trouble with both the church *and* the state. It's because you answer to a higher authority that doesn't appear in scripture or has yet to be enshrined in law. You follow the dictates of your conscience. It's a hard thing to defend and even more impossible to explain but you know that it's right. And just because there isn't anything to back it up now doesn't mean that there won't be one day. The world wasn't changed by strongmen and militants, but by the quiet, the humble, and the meek.

# LEO SUN/PISCES RISING

There's nothing low-key about you. You may think you're relaxed and easy-going, someone people can just hang out with, but it's not true. You are completely high maintenance. Even if you promise to sit there quietly, you'll still find a way to call attention to yourself. You might sigh audibly, turn the pages of a magazine loudly, or laugh raucously at some video you're watching on your smartphone. People often assume you do this because you're a Leo and Leos need to be the center of attention, but there's more to it than that. You're deathly afraid of disappearing. And it doesn't matter if you were the center of your parents' universe growing up—this fear of being left behind stubbornly remains. Calling attention to yourself in small and innocuous acts is your way of saying "I'm still here."

The reason for this has to do with your birth time—which is just after Sunset. This is when the Sun slips down beneath the horizon, taking the last gasp of day along with it. It's a challenging aspect for any horoscope because the Sun is as far away from the Ascendant as it can be, but it's especially difficult for you because the Sun is your Ruler. You can't help feeling like the light is leaving your life and that you're going to be left alone in the dark. It's why you're constantly checking in or following up. It's to make sure people are still where they said they would be.

Managing this kind of anxiety isn't easy, but it can be done by centering yourself in your body and getting in tune with your own rhythm. Yoga is a good idea because of the breath work, and swimming is another. These are physical disciplines that calm the mind.

In the end the only person who can reassure you is you, and the best way to do this is by being of service to others. It may seem strange seeking the company of people who are more messed up than you, but it has a remarkably calming effect by getting you to express those Leonine qualities of warmth and guidance. The more you instill confidence in others, the more you instill confidence in yourself, and the easier it becomes to bask in your own glow.

# VIRGO SUN/PISCES RISING

People often misread your willingness to help. Born under the zodiac sign of work and service, you are preprogrammed to lend a hand. You will go out of your way to help someone get back on their feet and—once done—you'll give them a hearty pat on the back and continue along your way. It's kind of like releasing an animal back into the wild. You assume that people in need will naturally pick up their lives again once they're over the hump. Unfortunately, the opposite is true.

You collect charity cases the way a robovac picks up dust. It's an occupational hazard for anyone with Pisces Rising. People see that you care. Even if you make a point of downplaying your concern, it still comes out in the questions you ask and the way that you listen. Moreover, your Pisces Rising casts this empathetic aura where people feel like they can tell you their problems in explicit detail. And it doesn't matter if you're in a hurry or are inundated with other pressing concerns, you will stop and listen to the whole sorry saga. What's worse is you'll even text them your number and invite them to keep in touch.

You've analyzed this foible of yours over and over again. Is it a need to please? Savior complex? Guilt? Actually, it comes from a place of selflessness; however, your Pisces Ascendant's idea of selflessness is different than your Virgo Sun's. Pisces is more universal in its approach. It has a collective "we're all in it together" mentality, which is two parts compassion and one part commiseration. It loves to feel the feelings. Virgos' selflessness is more utilitarian. Being an earth sign, Virgo recognizes the benefits of helping others because it helps you in the end. What gets lost in translation, however, is whether or not you even care. Most people don't see it, but intimates do.

It's why they're always asking if they really matter—and of course the more dutifully you respond, the more upset they become. Lovers, children, and friends want to feel like they are the top priority in your life—that they stand apart from everyone else. Hopefully one day you'll recognize the importance of this and when you do you'll give them good reason to stick around.

# LIBRA SUN/PISCES RISING

You have no idea what people see in you. When you look in the mirror you see someone who's rather ordinary; just another fish swimming in a school of like-minded souls. You don't think of yourself as a big catch, you aren't possessed by a driving ambition, and you really enjoy your own company. One of your favorite activities is getting lost. That might mean getting lost in a book, a favorite piece of music, or a city street you've never explored before. Your most precious moments are when nobody's around. It's when you're free to wander, meander, and drift.

Yet you have this knack for being in the wrong place at the right time for scandal. Like an innocent bystander found holding the knife, you pop up in situations where people can't help but assume the worst. Thankfully these don't involve murders, but they do include best friend's spouses trying to kiss you, supervisors confessing their romantic feelings, or love triangles where you had no idea that those two people were actually fighting over you. Loved ones and friends shoot skeptical glances because it's happened so many times. They no longer accept that you were just being nice. As a Libra/Pisces Rising it's impossible to say no. You don't want anyone to be hurt. Unfortunately it's by *not* saying no that you find yourself in these dilemmas.

You have to take responsibility for the effect you have. Your Pisces Ascendant casts a powerful spell and your Ruling Planet Venus (named after the Roman goddess of love and beauty) can't help but beguile, which is why it's up to you to tell people when you're not interested in them in that way. This isn't easy given that your Libra Sun wants to keep the door open and your Pisces Rising can't help wondering what if, but that's exactly what you need to do if you want to keep your friends and your job.

Finally, stop trying to fit into others' expectations. It's as much a figment of the imagination as what they project onto you. You know who you are when you're by yourself. That's why you like being alone and private. You need to bring that person into your everyday interactions. Life gets a lot easier when you're transparent instead of hidden behind some cloaking device.

# SCORPIO SUN/PISCES RISING

People love to gaze into your eyes. They have a calm, hypnotic effect. Indeed, being around you makes them feel uninhibited—like you get what they're really about. There's this feeling that their secrets are safe with you, that you understand feelings they barely understand themselves, and that they're free to say whatever they want because there's no judgment or fear of recrimination. It's really quite something the way others tell you things that they'd never share with a best friend or intimate partner. You're like a personal journal come to life, which is why they can't wait to confide in you what's been going on since last you met.

As you might imagine this doesn't always go over well with the people in that person's life. They might see you as a user or even a predator. They're suspicious of your motives and jealous of the bond you share. Yet you also won't do anything to assuage their apprehensions. Part of this stems from the fact that like a priest you're a closed book when it comes to someone's private confessions—you never betray them—but there's also a part of you that enjoys your special status, especially if the person confiding in you happens to be the boss's buddy, an ex's sibling, or a rival's spouse. Pisces/Scorpios often walk the line between fishy and foul, and although your Rising Sign describes the impression others have of you and not who you truly are, it's still not something to be treated casually. The world is full of confidantes who have been thrown under the bus when they overstayed their welcome or began to present an optics problem.

You care about people's spiritual lives and have a special affinity for those in crisis. Deeply religious—regardless of what faith you subscribe to—you've spent a lot of time in the lower depths. There's no way you could avoid it given Pisces's penchant for self-sabotage and Scorpio's craving for catharsis. These experiences have enriched you and bestowed a certain gravitas. People know you've been to hell and back, which is why they trust you. You can never save people from themselves, nor would you try to, but you will stand beside them on the ledge and be there for them when they want to climb down off of it.

## SAGITTARIUS SUN/PISCES RISING

You live a larger-than-life life. There's no holding back or playing it safe. You know that you were meant for great things and your aim is to experience each and every one of them. You have supreme confidence, an unshakable faith, and your ambition borders on hubris. It makes sense given that you were born at the time of day when the Sun is at its peak. Cap this off with Jupiter, the planet of good fortune, ruling both your Ascendant and Sun Sign and you're going to feel like nothing is beyond you. You famously believe your own hype and—much to the dismay of your rivals and competitors—your hype has never let you down.

It's hard to tell if you are so brimming with optimism that there's no room for doubt or if you really are as lucky as you say. Actually, it's both. Astrology books are full of cautionary tales about what happens to people who grow too big for their britches. They become egotistical, increasingly foolhardy, and prone to making mistakes. Thankfully none of this seems to affect you. Being born under Jupiter gives you a Teflon horoscope where the slings and arrows of outrageous fortune bounce off you like Superman staring down a barrage of bullets. And even if something bad were to happen, you always reemerge no worse for wear.

Sagittarius knows that we all come from the stars; that the fiery spirit that animates our body is here for a short duration. That's why there's a fierce recklessness to everything you do. It doesn't come from a feeling of invulnerability, but rather a deep-seated knowledge that nothing can harm you because you are made of star stuff and that once free of its mortal coil your spirit will return to the heavens where it belongs. This is something that your Pisces Rising—with its longing for higher planes and invisible worlds—can get behind and that's where you need to be careful. Those close calls and last-minute rescues aren't going to last forever, which begs the question: What's the rush? Take stock of your life and the wonderful people and places in it. It may not compare to the starry vault, but you may want to kick off your shoes and hang for a while.

## CAPRICORN SUN/PISCES RISING

You have the sort of cool and expressionless façade that hopeless romantics find captivating. The more you scowl, the more enraptured they become—convinced that they're the only ones who understand the heartbreak you carry around inside. That's why they're always speculating about your latest monosyllabic remark. For you it was a straightforward rebuff, but to them it betrayed a spark of interest, a fleeting sign of recognition, and maybe even a coded cry for help. It's amazing how much attention you generate for someone who wants to be left alone. And it's not just the people crushing on you who dog your every step. It's also the ones who are convinced that you are the answer to their prayers. There's something about you that emits depth and soulfulness. It's why people treat you like a sacred relic.

Capricorns are reluctant philosophers. You don't see yourself as especially wise or reflective. If anything, your life is dominated by work. Who has time to speculate if you're a person dreaming of being a butterfly or a butterfly dreaming of being a person when you have so many pressing deadlines? Yet your ability to describe esoteric concepts in the simplest language is what makes your reputation. You could be the lowest person on the corporate ladder and CEOs will still come to you for insight and advice. They see in you a font of knowledge that remains curiously unaware of itself, a unique combination of naivete and sagacity.

Higher-ups and people of influence play an enormous role in your life. They're the ones who champion your efforts and introduce you to friends who can open doors for you. It's all quite exciting except for this sinking feeling of indebtedness. Being a Capricorn/Pisces Rising you can't help but register every penny that's been spent on your behalf and you intend to pay it all back. It's a noble thought but impossible to honor given how much others will do for you. Capricorn/Pisces have a penchant for guilt. It's your favorite psychic hair shirt. And that's OK as long as you don't let guilt get in the way of gratitude. Instead of worrying about paying people back, try saying "thank you" instead. It goes a long way. One would think it had the power to make blind men see and the lame walk again.

# AQUARIUS SUN/PISCES RISING

It's hard to believe that you're for real. It's almost like you can read minds the way you intuit people's thoughts and emotions. Not only do you have your finger on the pulse of the room, but you can help those who aren't very good at articulating what they mean to find the right words to make their point. You're equally adept at appealing to the conscience of those who say they don't have one and getting them to think outside themselves and consider what's good for everyone involved. Equal parts empath and Vulcan, you can swing between heartfelt pleas and statistical analysis. Being an Aquarius/Pisces Rising means that you have a foot in both worlds.

You're often accused of disappearing. Your absences are so frequent that co-workers wonder if you might not be living a double life or feeding a drug habit. Their chronic complaint is that you can never be found when they need you, but somehow the job gets done. You may be late to the meeting or leave things to the last minute but what emerges is always something worth waiting for. That's why exceptions are made in your case when it comes to job performance. You'll never be voted employee of the month because of your tardiness, but any company that hires you knows that it will benefit from your foresight, creativity, and vision.

Yet there's a kind of madness that goes along with that genius when you're an Aquarius with Pisces Rising. You just can't resist sabotaging your own efforts. Whether it's taking unnecessary risks, flying too close to the sun, or being scattered at the time you need to be the most focused—there's a kind of built-in delight in watching things teeter on the brink right when they're about to come together. It's hard to tell if it stems from a fear of success or a fear that your freedom will be taken away if you are success-ful. In any case it's an impulse you need to tame or it will get the better of you.

Aquarius/Pisces Risings believe in benign neglect. You will never be on hand as much as others would like, but that doesn't mean you aren't work-ing behind the scenes to create the circumstances—and even the culture—for people to grow and thrive.

PART 3

# Face-to-Face:
# How Your Rising Sign
# Relates to Others

As you might imagine, the Rising Sign plays a strong role in any kind of relationship—whether it's romantic, professional, familial, or just friends. Most Astrology books talk about Sun Sign compatibility or the influence of the Moon, but none of these are going to come into play if you can't connect with another person's Ascendant. This first impression is the primary hook between horoscopes. If one person's Sun Sign isn't recognized by the other person's Rising Sign then there's nothing to draw them into each other's orbit. Here are the things you want to look for.

# WHEN YOUR SUN SIGN
# IS THEIR ASCENDENT

If your Sun Sign happens to be "rising" in the other person's chart—that is, you're a Leo Sun and the other person is a Leo Rising—then that's as good as gold. There's instant recognition, an easy rapport, and a bond that's hard to break.

# WHEN YOUR SUN SIGN AND
# THEIR ASCENDENT ARE THE SAME ELEMENT
# OR COMPLEMENTARY ELEMENTS

Let's say that you were born under Leo, a fire sign. This gives you an immediate affinity with the other two fire signs—Aries and Sagittarius. They're like family! The same goes for your complementary element—air. That means you'll get along breezily with Gemini and Libra. The one air Rising Sign where you will experience difficulty is Aquarius. That's because Leo is opposite Aquarius on the zodiacal wheel, which puts your Sun in the "setting" position of an Aquarius Rising's chart. This creates the feeling that you're always leaving, not around, or hard to get to know. The Sun in this position is as far away from the Ascendant as it can possibly be. This position is called the Descendant.

# WHEN YOUR SUN SIGN
# FLANKS THEIR RISING SIGN

If your Sun Sign happens to flank the other person's Rising Sign—that is, it's in the zodiac sign that immediately precedes or follows their Rising Sign—then this brings a closeness based on proximity. I have seen this show up in the charts of neighbors, co-workers, and even the barista who gets you your coffee order every morning. You may or may not be best pals, but you see each other on a daily basis and that's what this "proximity" is talking about.

Subsequently, your Sun Sign appearing in either of the zodiac signs that flanks the other person's Descendant shows that you don't really register. Now this doesn't mean your relationship is bad or ill-suited. It's more like the feeling of talking to someone who doesn't see you. It's no big deal because there are lots of people whom we look past every day on our way to work or standing in line at the supermarket checkout. Where this can be painful is when your Sun flanks the Descendant in a boss's or parent's chart. This creates a blind spot where it's hard for them to recognize your merits no matter how much others praise you.

Finally, where the Sun is in relation to another person's Ascendant describes how this person sees you. As mentioned earlier, your Sun near their Ascendant means that you're right next to them so they're going to see you as an equal. Your Sun above the horizon—like near the twelve noon point, for instance—means that they look up to you. Literally. Your Sun on the Descendant means you're leaving or not around, and your Sun below the horizon—near the midnight point—means that they look down on you.

Now that doesn't mean that they're being condescending. It's more like they see you as a fixture in their life. You're someone who will always be there for them.

As you read the following Rising Sign/Sun Sign combinations, try to keep in mind that these aren't meant to judge whether these are good or bad relationships, but rather meant to describe the *sticky* quality between one person's Sun Sign and another person's Rising Sign. Some combinations get each other right away while others will pass like ships in the night.

# IF YOU'RE AN ARIES RISING . . .

### AND THEY'RE ARIES:

You're like teammates. You have each other's backs. You're also healthy competitors who challenge each other to do better next time.

### AND THEY'RE TAURUS:

You don't mind that Taurus is stubborn. You're used to locking horns. What you mind is how slow they are. Methodical and deliberate, a Taurus will help you figure out how to build on what you have so that you're not always reinventing the wheel.

### AND THEY'RE GEMINI:

Talkers, not doers. Although their vocabulary is astonishing—how do they know so many words?—it's their genius for ducking out of things that's most impressive.

## AND THEY'RE CANCER:

Oversensitive! Everything you say and do hurts their feelings. You can't help feeling like you have to walk on eggshells when they're around.

## AND THEY'RE LEO:

Leos can read your heart. They're the ones you can talk to about the future and all the aspirations you're reluctant to share. They "get" the person you want to be.

## AND THEY'RE VIRGO:

Virgos are the perfect coaches, mentors, and tutors. They recognize your potential and want to help you realize it. The fact that you can never please them keeps you coming back for more.

## AND THEY'RE LIBRA:

This is the sign you have the most trouble with because they're so ambivalent. Libras are undoubtedly beautiful and appealing, but the fact that you never feel like a priority doesn't sit well with you.

## AND THEY'RE SCORPIO:

Scorpios are your Kryptonite. You share the same Ruling Planet (Mars) and you just can't keep your hands off them. However they hold grudges, whereas you don't, and fight dirty, which is something that gives you pause. You're not always sure if you trust them financially.

## AND THEY'RE SAGITTARIUS:

They're never around. This is great if it's a boss because you're free to do your own thing, not so good if you're romantically involved. The only sign that values their independence more than you, a Sagittarian will always open your world and broaden your horizons.

### AND THEY'RE CAPRICORN:

You want their love and respect so much that it hurts. This can lead to resentment as Capricorns can be withholding, but your passion eventually melts their façade. You just have to give this relationship a lot of time. There are ice ages that have moved faster.

### AND THEY'RE AQUARIUS:

You go in and out of each other's lives. Maybe you've been besties since childhood, worked for each other in different capacities over the years, or got together, broke up, only to get back together again. Yours is a lifelong on again/off again friendship.

### AND THEY'RE PISCES:

Your favorite damsel (or dude) in distress. You hate the way Pisces is always the victim, but that won't keep you from running into a burning building to rescue them.

# IF YOU'RE A TAURUS RISING . . .

### AND THEY'RE ARIES:

The unstoppable force to your immoveable object. That's why it's good to have a third party nearby who can help you work out your differences.

## AND THEY'RE TAURUS:

This is the one reliable person in your life.

## AND THEY'RE GEMINI:

They have this unique ability to transform what's formulaic into something fresh by tweaking a detail here or introducing a variation there.

## AND THEY'RE CANCER:

Things grow and prosper under your nurturing energies. These could be gardens, businesses, or children.

## AND THEY'RE LEO:

One of the best signs to settle down with. You get the house and they'll turn it into a castle.

## AND THEY'RE VIRGO:

You like being the breadwinner, but this can come across as too domineering for Virgos, who need to feel like they're contributing something. Leave them a bill or two to pay on their own and they'll be happy.

## AND THEY'RE LIBRA:

You come from two separate worlds: You're bargain basement while Libras are strictly couture. If you don't want your association to devolve into class warfare, then develop some respect for their stomping grounds while showing them what's fun about yours.

## AND THEY'RE SCORPIO:

It depends on the Scorpio. If they're constantly complaining about how life screws them over, then skip it. You don't need them tracking their muddy toxicity into your verdant pastures. If they're the type that's gone through hell and high water and can still laugh about it? You're all theirs.

## AND THEY'RE SAGITTARIUS:

There's a reason why the cowboy and the farmer don't get along. One's a rover and the other's a settler. Nevertheless, you're magic together on assignments and projects. Any production lucky enough to have you two working on it will be a success.

## AND THEY'RE CAPRICORN:

Your biggest challenge is getting a Capricorn to step away from the grindstone and spend some time with you. You'll succeed, but it will take a few tries. And you thought you were a workaholic?

## AND THEY'RE AQUARIUS:

An Aquarius will always get you to raise your sights. Maybe they're the teacher who saw something special in you, the coach who fostered your talent, or the spouse who wouldn't let you settle for less. They're all kinds of inspirational, but it would be nice if they'd just let up once in a while.

## AND THEY'RE PISCES:

You will always have a soft spot for Pisces. You're more generous with them than with any other sign, more forgiving and doting. Others complain about them getting preferential treatment and you wouldn't disagree.

# IF YOU'RE A GEMINI RISING . . .

**AND THEY'RE ARIES:**

It doesn't matter how many times you begin with "for the sake of argument," an Aries will always take it personally.

**AND THEY'RE TAURUS:**

Your secret accomplice. Not only do Taurus people know how to put those plans into action, but nobody would ever suspect them of being in on the shenanigans.

**AND THEY'RE GEMINI:**

Your frenemy. The good twin/bad twin dynamic is impossible to break, so it's nice to know that you can take turns.

**AND THEY'RE CANCER:**

They may not have two pennies to rub together at first, but stick with them because in time they'll wind up supporting you in the manner that you're accustomed to.

**AND THEY'RE LEO:**

You love pranking Leos. They're such easy targets! But the fact that they're so good humored about it teaches you the difference between laughing with someone versus laughing at them.

## AND THEY'RE VIRGO:

They're so uptight! But where would you be without someone to play parent to your mischievous child? Life wouldn't be half as fun without them.

## AND THEY'RE LIBRA:

It doesn't matter how hard you try, a Libra will always be classier than you. The best thing to do is stop trying to compete and learn from them instead.

## AND THEY'RE SCORPIO:

Scorpios mean it when they tell you to steer clear because you won't be able to handle them. If you're smart, you won't make them repeat it.

## AND THEY'RE SAGITTARIUS:

You're a lot alike even if you rub each other the wrong way. You can't help taking the piss out of a Sagittarius and they always overreact to anything you say. In time you can build a begrudging respect. You do best if you live on opposite coasts.

## AND THEY'RE CAPRICORN:

Your fights will always be over money. You want Capricorns to take care of your finances, but then criticize them for putting you on a budget. Things improve once you stop treating them like a parent doling out your weekly allowance.

## AND THEY'RE AQUARIUS:

The biggest revelation is when you discover that Aquarius people are goofier than you. This allows you to relax and really start to have some fun.

**AND THEY'RE PISCES:**

There's something about them that you admire. Maybe it's their depth, imagination, or ease with things that can't be easily explained. In any case you find them magical.

# IF YOU'RE A CANCER RISING . . .

**AND THEY'RE ARIES:**

Domineering and bossy. The best way to get along with an Aries is to let them do what they want and then circle back to salvage the situation afterward.

**AND THEY'RE TAURUS:**

Taurus people are wonderfully reassuring. They're more than happy to show you the ropes and don't mind repeating how to do something until you get it right.

**AND THEY'RE GEMINI:**

Like the proverbial younger sibling, they'll follow you around, say obnoxious things, and get into scrapes that you have to fish them out of. They're annoying but endearing. Works if it's a younger person, awkward if it's a boss.

**AND THEY'RE CANCER:**

An instant bond no matter how disparate your backgrounds. Your mannerisms and expressions are so similar that people will swear you're related.

## AND THEY'RE LEO:

A common pairing as your ruler is the Moon and Leo's is the Sun. One would think that you'd be like night and day, but you're not. You're the lamb that the lion wants to snuggle up next to.

## AND THEY'RE VIRGO:

A Virgo will say they like what you're doing and then tell you how you can improve on it. You have more patience for them than other signs do, which is why there are so many Virgos in your life.

## AND THEY'RE LIBRA:

Neither of you likes confrontation, which means you will leave it to the other one to broach an uncomfortable topic. Intimates are always pushing you to hash out your differences so that they don't have to hear about them at home.

## AND THEY'RE SCORPIO:

Scorpios are hopelessly devoted to you. Although they'll chastise you for being oversensitive, they still want to be the shoulder you cry on when you're going through a rough time.

## AND THEY'RE SAGITTARIUS:

You have a soft spot in your heart for this desperado sign. You will always take them back no matter how many times they disappoint or fail to deliver on their promises. You just know that they need to grow up and maybe one day they will.

**AND THEY'RE CAPRICORN:**

This is the stern parent you feel you can never please. And it doesn't matter if it's a three-year-old that you're dealing with—you'll still feel like a disappointment. It's hard to get over those childhood triggers, but Capricorns are in your life to help you do just that.

**AND THEY'RE AQUARIUS:**

Aquarians have a zero-tolerance policy when it comes to moodiness. It just doesn't register on their radar. Either speak up or prepare to be ignored.

**AND THEY'RE PISCES:**

You get each other on a deep and profound level, but sometimes you can't help wondering what they're doing with their lives. They're just so adrift.

# IF YOU'RE A LEO RISING . . .

**AND THEY'RE ARIES:**

They won't let you rest on your laurels. Aries is always looking for a way to raise the bar or up the ante. They're the reason you're still in great shape at fifty.

**AND THEY'RE TAURUS:**

Things get better when you're around this sign. Your quality of life improves, your confidence soars, and you feel more secure. However, neither one of you will back down in a fight so you need to practice your apologies.

### AND THEY'RE GEMINI:

Geminis are good at getting you to question familiar assumptions and experiment. The end result is that you grow in unexpected ways.

### AND THEY'RE CANCER:

Cancers are your emotional comfort zone. You've been turning to them for love and support since childhood. This is the sign you can be the most yourself with.

### AND THEY'RE LEO:

Instantly simpatico. There's no missing that solar spark. But can your egos coexist? You need to decide who's lead vocalist and who's singing backup to make this relationship work.

### AND THEY'RE VIRGO:

It's a Virgo's job to point out all the things you missed. Once you accept that they're doing this to make you a better person (and not to bring you down), then yours will be a productive partnership.

### AND THEY'RE LIBRA:

The best sign to take selfies with. Because they're well-read and conversational, you can enter a room with confidence as long as a Libra's on your arm. They always make you look (and sound) good.

### AND THEY'RE SCORPIO:

You're like a dog drawn to a cat. And it doesn't matter how many times you're hissed at or get your nose scratched, you'll keep coming back for more.

### AND THEY'RE SAGITTARIUS:

The perfect relationship for when you're between relationships because nobody's better at climbing back on the horse that threw them like a Sagittarius. You'll have a great time as long as it lasts.

### AND THEY'RE CAPRICORN:

Capricorns are like a sitcom dad. They practically come equipped with cardigan sweaters and smoking pipes.

### AND THEY'RE AQUARIUS:

You either click or you don't. Since it's always a fifty-fifty prospect, it's best to approach Aquarians on a case-by-case basis.

### AND THEY'RE PISCES:

It's the disappearing act that troubles you most. Pisces need to retreat from the world from time to time—and that includes a break from you too. Give them their space and they'll eventually reappear.

# IF YOU'RE A VIRGO RISING . . .

### AND THEY'RE ARIES:

You can't help holding back. Whether it's your approval or support, it's hard to believe that an Aries person will stay. It's why you keep your distance. If you don't want this to become a self-fulfilling prophecy then work on building trust.

## AND THEY'RE TAURUS:

One of the few signs you can be yourself with. You don't feel labeled or judged. They totally understand your need to pick things apart. Perhaps the best thing about Taurus is their easygoing nature. Spend enough time with them and that relaxed quality will rub off on you.

## AND THEY'RE GEMINI:

You always feel like Geminis get away with things that others don't—and you're right: They do. But instead of focusing on what's wrong, borrow a page from their playbook. You could learn a lot.

## AND THEY'RE CANCER:

You totally get each other. You often talk about how simple life would be if only you felt an attraction. Hopefully that will come with time. If not? Then what you gain instead is a best friend for life.

## AND THEY'RE LEO:

You're an expert lion tamer. You can tell when to feed, coddle, or crack the whip. Others worry about you playing second fiddle, but you know you're the real power behind the throne.

## AND THEY'RE VIRGO:

You're like two champion chess players who can anticipate each other's moves. Not the easiest relationship to have when you're younger—the one-upmanship is nonstop—but it makes for a wonderful pairing later on because it fits comfortably, like a favorite cardigan sweater.

## AND THEY'RE LIBRA:

Yours is a dangerous combination. Given your eye for detail and Libra's gift for packaging, you two could clean up in whatever endeavor you pursued together.

## AND THEY'RE SCORPIO:

You enjoy fighting each other's battles. A Scorpio can always rely on you to dig up that piece of information they need to win the day, while you know that if anyone gives you trouble then all you have to do is text your Scorpio friend and they'll take care of it.

## AND THEY'RE SAGITTARIUS:

You hate how Sagittarians can pick up on the one thing you're not saying and expose it for the hidden hurt or resentment that it is. It's like a parent catching you sneaking out of the house at night. You've no choice but to fess up.

## AND THEY'RE CAPRICORN:

You'll never meet their standards. It's why you're nervous about disappointing them. However, this self-consciousness could get in the way of an enormously creative collaboration. Focus more on learning than proving and you'll benefit from a Capricorn's sagacity and support.

## AND THEY'RE AQUARIUS:

Twin perfectionists, you pride yourselves on efficiency. It's why you're often paired together at work. Terrific at tackling tough projects, you do best under tight deadlines. Too much time in each other's company makes you agitated and nitpicky.

### AND THEY'RE PISCES:

You keep trying to solve this person's problems. Did it ever occur to you that they like their problems? Your matter-of-fact approach to life doesn't mix well with their longing for things they can never have.

# IF YOU'RE A LIBRA RISING . . .

### AND THEY'RE ARIES:

Equal parts exasperating and exhilarating. They say that opposites attract, but they don't always stay together. You need a lot of spaces in your togetherness.

### AND THEY'RE TAURUS:

One of the few signs that really gets you because you're both slow to make up your minds. Taurus has no problem with you taking all the time that you need—as long as it doesn't cost extra.

### AND THEY'RE GEMINI:

Why are you always accused of vacillating when Geminis make and then unmake decisions all the time? You've never met a sign fonder of loopholes and escape clauses. Ironically this allows you to grow close.

### AND THEY'RE CANCER:

Cancers mean serious business. They often materialize as authority figures in your life and occasionally even spouses. You hold each other in high esteem and are careful not to hurt the other one's feelings.

## AND THEY'RE LEO:

No other sign is committed to you being you. It's true that the Leo ego can be hard to bear, but they're true to themselves in a way that inspires you to do the same. Over time their audacity rubs off.

## AND THEY'RE VIRGO:

Virgos and Libras have a lot in common. You're both cerebral, stylish, and born perfectionists. Unfortunately, Virgos like being told what to do, and Libras are shy about barking orders.

## AND THEY'RE LIBRA:

This is a great combination because you're both on the same page about your relationship. And it doesn't matter what kind of incarnations it goes through—friends, lovers, business partners, joint custody—being in each other's lives and finding a way to make it work always comes first.

## AND THEY'RE SCORPIO:

Be very careful around this sign. They can bring a lot of money to the table when you get together, but they'll cost even more if you part ways.

## AND THEY'RE SAGITTARIUS:

Sagittarians often complain about you not taking them seriously, which is OK because they don't take you seriously either.

## AND THEY'RE CAPRICORN:

Capricorns are your rock. They may not be able to keep up with you when it comes to working the social circuit—they're horrible at remembering faces, names, and labels—but they're your favorite people to come home to at the end of the day.

### AND THEY'RE AQUARIUS:

Aquarians are always changing the rules on you and this can be quite befuddling. However, if you stick with them long enough you will probably discover that those rules were long overdue for an upgrade—and that you have grown as a result.

### AND THEY'RE PISCES:

You're poetic souls. You both respond to music, film, and art. The nice thing about being around a Pisces is that they get you to experiment and push the boundaries. The hardest? They're loud and thundering when they get upset. Thankfully you know how to make yourself scarce.

## IF YOU'RE A SCORPIO RISING . . .

### AND THEY'RE ARIES:

People assume you're together. That's because you joke, bicker, and defend one another like any couple would. You're besties and rivals for life.

### AND THEY'RE TAURUS:

Great to look at but all that changes when they open their mouth . . .

## AND THEY'RE GEMINI:

Geminis always want to be best friends. You tried that back in college. People try a lot of things in college. You know better now.

## AND THEY'RE CANCER:

Cancers make you feel loved and adored. They're like the favorite aunt you can never disappoint. They're the only ones allowed to give you a nickname.

## AND THEY'RE LEO:

You put them on a pedestal. You can't help it. And it doesn't matter how many times they disappoint, fall on their face, or drop the ball—you will still stand by them.

## AND THEY'RE VIRGO:

Your "inside man." They show up as your crush's bestie, your boss's cousin, or the person who walks the dogs for that client you're trying to score. Virgos provide access to those you wouldn't have met otherwise.

## AND THEY'RE LIBRA:

Your favorite obsession. Libras are your agony *and* your ecstasy.

## AND THEY'RE SCORPIO:

Scorpios are like a mirror. If you have a healthy self-image then you couldn't ask for a better companion. If not? Then you will project all the things you don't like about yourself onto them.

### AND THEY'RE SAGITTARIUS:

Don't leave them alone in the same room with your credit card.

### AND THEY'RE CAPRICORN:

The best sign to have fun with. You're like schoolgirls with your knees pressed together sharing secrets and giggling hysterically. People always ask you what you're laughing about but you'll never tell.

### AND THEY'RE AQUARIUS:

Aquarians are intellectually detached. You are too personally invested. It shouldn't work, but it does. Only someone as hardheaded as yourself can challenge you to see things in ways you never would have appreciated before.

### AND THEY'RE PISCES:

They will always be unicorns to you. Rare, magical, and mysterious beings who are terminally tardy—like when they showed up late for the Ark, long after the doors had closed.

# IF YOU'RE A SAGITTARIUS RISING . . .

### AND THEY'RE ARIES:

Passion brings you together, but fighting can drive you apart. You feel like Aries has anger-management issues and Aries feels like you OVERREACT to everything.

## AND THEY'RE TAURUS:

A great creative collaborator—especially on short-term projects. Anything longer than that and you grow bored with their routine and begin to resent their bossiness.

## AND THEY'RE GEMINI:

You can never tell if they really like you or not. Sometimes it feels like they're putting up with you until the person they really want to talk to comes along.

## AND THEY'RE CANCER:

Cancers are like Mom. They may never get what you're about, but they're always the ones you come home to no matter where you've been.

## AND THEY'RE LEO:

You envy how Leos step into leadership positions like they were born to it. You wish that you were that comfortable with exercising authority.

## AND THEY'RE VIRGO:

You like being corrected by a Virgo. They have a special talent for identifying what you're doing wrong and showing you how to do better next time. It's the only sign you let talk to you like that.

## AND THEY'RE LIBRA:

Always gracious and welcoming, they'll act as if they've never heard mention of you when being introduced, but they're quite familiar with your reputation. It's why they agreed to meet in the first place.

### AND THEY'RE SCORPIO:

Scorpio's darkness doesn't get you down. Maybe it's because your optimism truly is impervious or your ability to hit the bull's-eye with a targeted remark is just as precise. In any case, Scorpios know they've met their match with you.

### AND THEY'RE SAGITTARIUS:

Always up for an adventure! Your favorite pal to go camping and/or zip-lining with.

### AND THEY'RE CAPRICORN:

At first they'll say that your idea is ludicrous, but gradually they'll recognize that it has merit. Of course, what they turn it into has nothing to do with what you had in mind, but that won't stop you from taking credit for its success.

### AND THEY'RE AQUARIUS:

Both of you are into changing the world and will certainly give it your best shot. This is a bond that should work, but at the end of the day Aquarians are too cold—even for you.

### AND THEY'RE PISCES:

You're like twins separated at birth who have been miraculously reunited. It takes a while to figure out what kind of relationship you want to have, but that won't stop you from trying on all the different hats.

# IF YOU'RE A CAPRICORN RISING . . .

**AND THEY'RE ARIES:**

They always show up at the times that matter—like when you're at a critical juncture or feel like you have lost your way. They may not stay long, but their impact is fundamental.

**AND THEY'RE TAURUS:**

The least neurotic of the earth signs, you could benefit from Taurus's worry-free relationship to finances. If they want something, they buy it. They're that confident in their earning power. This is the sign that gets you to take the money out of the mattress and to do something fun with it instead.

**AND THEY'RE GEMINI:**

You know there's more going on beneath the surface. It's just hard to imagine what that might be.

**AND THEY'RE CANCER:**

You hate how shamelessly sentimental this sign can be, but you would miss them if they weren't around.

**AND THEY'RE LEO:**

You often assume that Leos have it easier than you, but they don't. Yes, they may look like a million bucks, but you have no idea of the price they pay for upkeep.

## AND THEY'RE VIRGO:

You have a secret thing for Virgos. There's something about the servant/master dynamic that turns you on. It's very *Downton Abbey*. With safe words.

## AND THEY'RE LIBRA:

Yours is a competitive relationship, but it doesn't have to be. The sooner you come clean about your admiration for Libra's refined tastes, the sooner the Libra will reciprocate with praise for your hard-won achievements.

## AND THEY'RE SCORPIO:

Scorpios show you how success is won. Not only will they have those talks with you that nobody else can have, but they are fiercely committed to you making something of yourself.

## AND THEY'RE SAGITTARIUS:

The only one who can convince you that the glass is half full when you already know it's half empty.

## AND THEY'RE CAPRICORN:

People know better than to interrupt when you're talking to each other. Your hushed tones and concentrated expressions broadcast that it's serious business.

## AND THEY'RE AQUARIUS:

It takes a long time to get together, but when you do, it's solid.

**AND THEY'RE PISCES:**

You will always be grateful that it was a Pisces who introduced themselves first when you were hugging the wall in preschool—and Pisces have been the icebreakers since, be it a high-school mixer, a dinner party, or a corporate function.

# IF YOU'RE AN AQUARIUS RISING . . .

**AND THEY'RE ARIES:**

One of the best allies you could hope for. They may not understand what you're talking about half the time, but they'll support you just the same.

**AND THEY'RE TAURUS:**

They always say that what you're planning will never work, but give them enough time and they'll figure out a way to make it happen.

**AND THEY'RE GEMINI:**

Geminis look up to you. That's because you can see further down the road than they can, and you're unpredictable enough to keep them guessing.

**AND THEY'RE CANCER:**

The perfect workmate. Cancers are really good at smoothing over the bruised egos and ruffled feathers you often leave in your wake.

## AND THEY'RE LEO:

Yes, they take up a lot of time and attention, but so do children and family pets.

## AND THEY'RE VIRGO:

Your go-to source for inside tips, office gossip, and brief explanations for hard-to-grasp technical concepts. More than just know-it-alls, Virgos will actually show you how to do what you want to do.

## AND THEY'RE LIBRA:

Although often paired together at work or as charades partners, there's not much that locks you into each other's orbit. The interest may be passing, but you're always cordial and professional.

## AND THEY'RE SCORPIO:

Scorpios either come into your life during a crisis or because they *are* the crisis. In any case there's no disputing the transformative impact they have on your life.

## AND THEY'RE SAGITTARIUS:

You're both freedom-loving signs and hit it off when there's a cause that inspires you or an outrage that unites you, but in truth Sagittarians are a bit too wild for you. While you're looking for ways to bring disaffected parties back to the table, a Sagittarius is busy pouring gasoline on the fire.

## AND THEY'RE CAPRICORN:

They're like the straitlaced sibling nobody would ever guess is related to you. Nevertheless, they're the ones you turn to for advice and support.

**AND THEY'RE AQUARIUS:**

It's hard for others to follow your conversation. Not only do you speak at the speed of telepathic thought, but so much is intrinsically understood that you rarely have to explain yourself. You're perfectly in sync until you're not.

**AND THEY'RE PISCES:**

Your signs are naturally close, yet something always comes up to keep you at a distance. Even if you're in a relationship you'll spend a lot of time apart because of conflicting schedules.

# IF YOU'RE A PISCES RISING . . .

**AND THEY'RE ARIES:**

You spend a lot of time talking about money. Probably because neither of you is good with it. Hopefully there's a mutual friend or in-law who's an accountant.

**AND THEY'RE TAURUS:**

You learned a long time ago that if you sit attentively through the life lectures and nod in all the right places then a Taurus will do anything for you.

**AND THEY'RE GEMINI:**

You disagree more than you agree and can get into lengthy debates. People often mistake the bickering for arguing, but that's not the case. This person is like family and will always take your side if need be.

## AND THEY'RE CANCER:

You're a natural fit. You can hang out for days and never grow tired of each other's company. This is your favorite person to share a song, a Sunset, or an inside joke with. They always get it.

## AND THEY'RE LEO:

Leos mean well, but just don't understand. Explaining your take on things or how you arrived at a certain conclusion always leaves them feeling confused, which is why it's easier just to change the subject. That said, they're great workmates.

## AND THEY'RE VIRGO:

You can't quite remember where the Virgo in your life got the impression that you can't get along without them. They always feel like they know more than you and that you can benefit from their guidance. The opposite is true, but you won't say anything. You don't want to hurt their feelings.

## AND THEY'RE LIBRA:

You could be neighbors for years and never have a conversation. Always happy to greet each other with a smile or a pleasant "How are you doing?"— but there isn't much interest in taking things any further.

## AND THEY'RE SCORPIO:

This is the person you're on the phone with till all hours of the night helping them with their problems and plights. You know that they'll never take your advice, but that doesn't stop you from offering it anyway.

## AND THEY'RE SAGITTARIUS:

One of your favorite signs! They're always so happy and upbeat! It's true that they have all the personal sensitivity of a birthday party clown, but you've more than enough melancholy to go around. Their default solution to any problem is a change of scene and you're down with that.

## AND THEY'RE CAPRICORN:

One of the few people who will ask you about you. Now that could be because you're running late or look a mess, but at least they care. Not the ideal person to break down in front of, but after sitting there in polite silence they're sure to offer a solution to your troubles.

## AND THEY'RE AQUARIUS:

It's the tough times that bring you together. Episodes that would have driven others apart only strengthen your bond.

## AND THEY'RE PISCES:

Your favorite enabler. You can count on a Pisces to slip you the cigarette, a sip, or a toke. Yes, they encourage behaviors that shouldn't always be encouraged, but when it's time to stop cold they'll be there for you.

# Face Value:
# The Self behind the Selfie

As children we're told not to judge a book by its cover, yet civilizations have been doing this for centuries. Indeed, the Rising Sign in Astrology has long been associated with physiognomy—the ancient art of judging someone's character by their physical appearance. It was a given that every body possessed a soul, but physiognomists believed that as the body grew, so did its inner soul—shaping its face and demeanor, making its personality identifiable for everyone to see. In many ways, physiognomists were the world's first psychologists, diagnosing behavior according to someone's individual features and mannerisms. Many Astrology books continue that practice to this day when they say Leo Risings have magnificent manes, Sagittarius Risings are horse-faced, and those with Aries on the Ascendant are red-haired and quarrelsome—like their planetary ruler Mars, the god of war. Unfortunately, over time, the personality profiling championed by physiognomy devolved into biased judgments and racist stereotypes.

This is why it's wise not to take things at face value. But what about the value of the face?

Back in the late 1990s when email was a thing and people were using it for personal and professional correspondence—as well as in chat rooms—it became clear quite quickly that it wasn't always easy to read another person's tone. A brisk message might be regarded as a cutting remark, a wordy post was condescending, or a critical note felt overly harsh and uncalled for. With no face or voice to accompany them, emails were read according to whatever mood or mind-set the recipient happened to be in. If one was feeling anxious or insecure, then all of that got projected onto an email—no matter how innocuous. This led to the insertion of symbols like :-), ;-), and :-0 as well as LOLs, IMHOs, and <3s. Forerunners of the emoji, these symbols and acronyms were meant to comment on a text in the way a facial expression would by injecting humor, reassurance, or humility. When met with facelessness, it was only human nature to make a face up.

Ancient Astrologers felt the same way about horoscopes. Horoscopes needed a face just like a person does. That's why it's not the birthday that distinguishes a chart's uniqueness—lots of people can be born on the same day and share the same general characteristics—but rather the birth hour that binds an astrological chart exclusively to its owner. In fact, the word *horoscope* means "hour watcher."

Without a Rising Sign, our birth charts would be directionless. There would be no sense of up and down or right and left. There would be no start or end, no motivation or priority. The Rising Sign is square one in a horoscope—it's the first step you take, the first impression you make, and the zodiac sign that leads all the others. So not only is it the face you show the world, the Rising Sign also describes how you face the world.

The most important planet in your horoscope is the Sun. It is who you are and were always meant to be; however, it's the Rising Sign that tells us where the Sun was in the sky when you were born. Is it above or below the horizon? Is it near the Ascendant or far away? The Sun's proximity to the Rising Sign tells you if you're comfortable in your own skin or if it will take a while to grow into who you really are. Are you meant to rise above a situation or do you need to dig down deep into yourself to unearth the hidden treasures you didn't know you had?

Finally, we all need to understand how we come across to others. That self-awareness is a vital aspect of being a functional human being. No one's a human being in a vacuum. And that's where the Rising Sign takes precedence over the Sun. Smiles, laughter, averted gazes, and bored expressions signal whether you're getting warmer or colder in a conversation. Interpreting these faces is paramount to courting a mate, negotiating a sale, or managing a group of people. In this regard, how we read a room has replaced tracking animal footprints when it comes to our survival.

For some people, this ability to read others as well as themselves is organic and chances are the relationship between the Sun Sign and Rising Sign in their birth chart reflects that. But for those of us who feel thrust into situations that we didn't choose, struggle with inhibitions we find hard to explain, or work to reconcile the person others see with the person we really are—the Rising Sign is something we need to know better. No one goes through life as an authentic person by accident. That's the product of an ongoing creative collaboration between your Sun Sign and Ascendant. Being true to yourself isn't a solo effort—especially when others may have a higher vision of you than you have of yourself.

# ACKNOWLEDGMENTS

I want to thank Megan Newman, my publisher; Lisa DiMona, my agent; Marian Lizzi, my editor; and Natasha Soto. These are the people every writer dreams of working with.

And where would an astrologer be without his constellations? I want to thank the guiding lights who have shaped my vision and my voice: Deborah Schatten, Coco Fusco, Catherine Karnow, Lindsay McCrum, Debbie Millman, Gwen Sutton, and Gregory Nassif St. John.

**Christopher Renstrom** is the author of *The Cosmic Calendar* and *Ruling Planets*, and the creator of rulingplanets.com. He currently writes the daily horoscopes for SFGate.com, along with the weekly horoscope for Astrology Hub. He also lectures on the history of astrology in America from pre-Revolution to modern times, and runs Ruling Planets workshops around the country.

Also by

# CHRISTOPHER RENSTROM

THE COSMIC
CALENDAR

Using Astrology to Get in Sync with Your Best Life

CHRISTOPHER RENSTROM